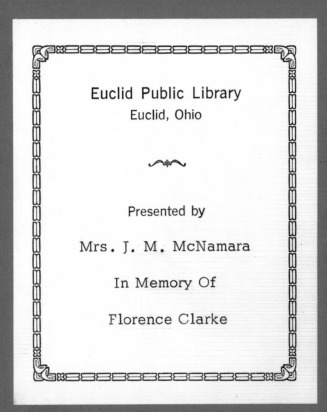

Yesterday's Cleveland

Seemann's Historic Cities Series

No. 1: *Yesterday's Tampa* by Hampton Dunn
No. 2: *Yesterday's Miami* by Nixon Smiley
No. 3: *Yesterday's St. Petersburg* by Hampton Dunn
No. 4: *Yesterday's Key West* by Stan Windhorn & Wright Langley
No. 5: *Yesterday's Sarasota* by Del Marth
No. 6: *Yesterday's Clearwater* by Hampton Dunn
No. 7: *Yesterday's Tallahassee* by Hampton Dunn
No. 8: *Yesterday's Atlanta* by Franklin M. Garrett
No. 9: *Yesterday's Detroit* by Frank Angelo
No. 10: *Yesterday's Denver* by Sandra Dallas
No. 11: *Yesterday's Cape Cod* by Evelyn Lawson
No. 12: *Yesterday's Florida Keys* by Stan Windhorn & Wright Langley
No. 13: *Yesterday's Philadelphia* by George Wilson
No. 14: *Yesterday's Akron* by Kenneth Nichols
No. 15: *Yesterday's Fort Myers* by Marian Godown & Alberta Rawchuck
No. 16: *Yesterday's Nashville* by Carl Zibart
No. 17: *Yesterday's Asheville* by Joan & Wright Langley
No. 18: *Yesterday's Birmingham* by Malcolm C. McMillan
No. 19: *Yesterday's Cincinnati* by Luke Feck
No. 20: *Yesterday's Bradenton* by Arthur C. Schofield
No. 21: *Yesterday's San Diego* by Neil Morgan & Tom Blair
No. 22: *Yesterday's Chicago* by Herman & Rick Kogan
No. 23: *Yesterday's Milwaukee* by Robert W. Wells
No. 24: *Yesterday's Washington, D. C.* by Charles Ewing
No. 25: *Yesterday's Memphis* by Charles W. Crawford
No. 26: *Yesterday's Los Angeles* by Norman Dash
No. 27: *Yesterday's Augusta* by Ray Rowland & Helen Callahan
No. 28: *Yesterday's Lexington* by Eric Karnes
No. 29: *Yesterday's Palm Beach* by Stuart McIver
No. 30: *Yesterday's Cleveland* by George E. Condon

GEORGE E. CONDON

Yesterday's
CLEVELAND

Seemann's Historic Cities Series No. 30

E. A. Seemann Publishing, Inc.
Miami, Florida

Many individuals and institutions have kindly supported the author's task in collecting photographs for this book. Their invaluable help is gratefully acknowledged. All photographs without an abbreviated credit at the end of the caption come from the collection of the author; all others were contributed or photographed by the following (all located in Cleveland):

Ambrose	Charles Ambrose Collection	Helms	H. J. Helms Photo
Baus	Louis Baus Photo	Kraffert	Andrew J. Kraffert Collection
Bell	Ohio Bell Telephone Company	Marcell	Marcell Studio
Brumbach	Dudley Brumbach	Meli	James Meli Photo
Burke	Robert E. Burke Photo	Murway	A. K. Murway Collection
Butler	Clyde H. Butler Photo	News	*Cleveland News*
CAC	Cleveland Automobile Club	Plain Dealer	*Cleveland Plain Dealer*
C&O	Cheseapeake & Ohio Railway Company	Rebman	Herb Rebman Photo
Carroll	Peter Carroll Photo	Reeves	H. H. Reeves Photo
CEIC	Cleveland Electric Illuminating Company	Seid	Herman Seid Collection
		Sohio	Sohio News Service
		Wager	Richard Wager Collection
CFD	Cleveland Fire Department	WGAR	WGAR Radio
City	City of Cleveland	White	White Motor Corporation and White Products Company
CPL	Cleveland Public Library, History Division, Cleveland Picture Collection	WHK	WHK Radio
		Wilk	Charles Wilk Collection, Chessie System
Condon	Maurice J. Condon Photo		
Cragg	Perry Cragg Photo	WRHS	Western Reserve Historical Society
CTR	Cleveland Transit System	WTAM	WTAM Radio
Edmondson	George M. Edmondson Photo	Yassanye	Norbert Yassanye Photo
EOG	East Ohio Gas Company		

Library of Congress Cataloging in Publication Data

Condon, George E
  Yesterday's Cleveland.

  (Seemann's historic cities series ; no. 30)
  Includes index.
  1. Cleveland--History--Pictorial works. 2. Cleveland
--Description--Views. I. Title.
F499.C643C66   977.1'32'00222   76-21243
ISBN 0-912458-73-9

COPYRIGHT   1976 by George E. Condon
Library of Congress Catalog Card Number 76-21243
ISBN 0-912458-73-9

Manufactured in the United States of America.

For my sisters
The Formidable Four:
Ellen, Anne, Mary, and Kathleen

Contents

Acknowledgments / 9

In the Beginning: 1796 / 11

Cleveland from 1796 to 1825 / 15

Cleveland from 1825 to 1850 / 19

Cleveland from 1850 to 1875 / 23

Cleveland from 1875 to 1900 / 35

Cleveland from 1900 to 1925 / 55

Cleveland from 1925 to 1950 / 93

Index / *141*

Acknowledgments

THERE ARE ALWAYS hundreds of helping hands in the preparation of any book, too many to identify by name. I would like to acknowledge, though, the cooperation and assistance of those persons whose contributions were especially valuable.

Special thanks for their generous cooperation is owed to Thomas Vail, publisher and editor of *The Cleveland Plain Dealer,* and to Thomas Guthrie, executive editor of the *Plain Dealer.* Others I would like to thank are Miss Grace Parch, director of the library of the *Plain Dealer,* and her aides, Paul Rowland, Nancy Gardner, and Mary Jane Grabenstetter; Richard Misch, *Plain Dealer* photographer; Herman Seid, photographer, formerly with *The Cleveland News* and *The Cleveland Press*; Milton Dolinger, assistant vice president for public relations, The Chessie System; Miss Peggy Wardin, in charge of historical pictures in the History Department, Cleveland Public Library; Kermit Pike, director of the Western Reserve Historical Society Library; Miss Betty Royon of Acadia Farms, Northfield, Ohio; Bernie Butler, Sohio public relations; Craig Thompson, White Motor Corporation, public relations; and Alfred K. Murway, public relations director, Cleveland Automobile Club.

George E. Condon

Cleveland, Ohio

OHIO'S COMPONENT PARTS are many. The comparative size of Connecticut's Western Reserve, of which Cleveland was the first settlement, is shown in the above map. (Plain Dealer)

In the Beginning: 1796

CLEVELAND is an integral part of Ohio. It is, in fact, the largest, wealthiest, most populous, and most influential city in the state. But that is only the surface city, the present metropolis, the end product of time. There is another dimension to this great cluster of humanity on the shore of Lake Erie, and it is to be found only in the history records, written and pictorial.

Cleveland, for all its Midwestern gloss, is an outgrowth of New England. Its roots go deep and travel far; some five hundred miles to the east, all the way to Connecticut.

The family resemblance is still there. It is apparent in the New England look that is unmistakably a part of so many neighborhoods and satellite communities; in the impressive rollcall of names so familiar to Eastern society; and in the common customs and traditions that still persist after more than a century and half.

When the Revolutionary War ended, the Congress of the United States, no doubt with a heavy sigh, set about the onerous task of untangling a snarl of territorial claims that threatened to tie up several states of the newly formed union in boundary feuds of a seriously disruptive nature.

One such claim had little Connecticut reaffirming its title to a vast, unmeasured strip of land extending from the western edge of Pennsylvania all the way across the continent to California. This was patently a most unrealistic extension of the Nutmeg State, but the leaders of Connecticut were reasonable men and shrewd realists. They settled their claim for something less—but something, still, of considerable value.

The United States Government reserved for Connecticut a 120-mile strip of land bordering the southern shoreline of Lake Erie, all the way from Pennsylvania to a point, just west of Sandusky, deep in the Ohio country. This enormous tract became known as the Western Reserve of Connecticut.

It was unspoiled, unsullied, virgin territory. Some of the greatest forests the world ever has known covered most of the land, and no matter what paths the earliest explorers followed, their reports were in agreement: The ground was fertile, the brooks and streams ran clear, game abounded, and Lake Erie was a crystal delight. Every prospect in the Ohio country was pleasing. The red man had been a careful custodian of the western paradise.

There were more than three million acres in the Western Reserve, and some in Hartford dreamt of shaping the area into an independent state. The name of New Connecticut was bandied about as a possibility. It was an appealing idea.

More appealing to the most influential state leaders, however, was the idea of selling the western real estate to enrich Connecticut's treasury, and that practical approach prevailed over the dreams of the visionaries.

In 1795, Connecticut agreed to sell the part of its Western Reserve which extended as far west as the Cuyahoga River to a syndicate of investors called the Connecticut Land Company for a price of $1 million. The cost to the purchasers was approximately fifty-seven cents an acre.

Among the fifty-seven investors in the syndicate was a swarthy, stocky, gruff individual named Moses Cleaveland. From all accounts, Cleaveland was a man with an executive flair: the kind of man who usually is described as a natural leader. These qualities, and the fact that he had elected to risk some $32,600 of his own money in the big land speculation, caused the company to charge him with a heavy responsibility.

The millions of acres in the Ohio country were worthless until they could be surveyed. After that preliminary, the land could be resold to settlers at a profit. Cleaveland was appointed general agent of the Connecticut Land Company and was named to head a surveying expedition into the western territory. At the same time, the Connecticut legislature, in a move no doubt intended to bolster Cleaveland's prestige and authority, named him a brigadier general in the state militia.

In June 1796, the survey party left Connecticut on a mission that would open up a large tract of the American wilderness and select the site of a city of the future.

On July 4, 1796, the Cleaveland party reached the Pennsylvania boundary and crossed over into the Connecticut Western Reserve, stopping to pitch camp at the side of Coniaught Creek, later the site of Conneaut.

The next day, the group split into four separate surveying parties to undertake the staggering job of measuring the wilderness and partitioning it. Cleaveland himself, with a hand-picked group, drove on westward towards the Cuyahoga River by way of Lake Erie, finally arriving at his destination, the mouth of the river, on July 22, 1796.

THE CONNECTICUT YANKEE who gave Cleveland its name was Gen. Moses Cleaveland, an investor in the Connecticut Land Company purchase of some three million acres in the Western Reserve, from the Pennsylvania border to the Cuyahoga River. General Cleaveland led the company's surveying expedition into the Ohio wilderness in 1796 and selected the site for the future city. He is shown in this oil portrait by a Cleveland artist, E. Ladislaw Novotney, who was commissioned to do the work by the Federal Public Works Program during the Depression. (Plain Dealer)

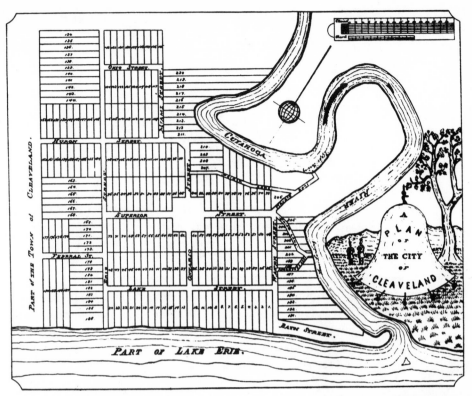

THE SURVEYING PARTY under Moses Cleaveland that staked out the first settlement in the Western Reserve camped on the east bank of the Cuyahoga River only about three months in 1796, but out of that brief stay emerged the first plan of Cleveland, as drawn up by Seth Pease, a surveyor and one of General Cleaveland's aides. An outline of the heart of the modern city is still to be found in the prophetic tracing.

Here, as the councils of the land company had predetermined, would be the site of the first settlement in New Connecticut. Its name also had been decided: Cleaveland.

How "Cleaveland" evolved into "Cleveland" is not entirely clear. The favorite explanation is that a printer-editor simplified the spelling. It is more likely that people simply chose the easier, not uncommon, spelling of the old family name.

The doughty band of Connecticut pioneers did not find the site of Cleveland to be the kind of place that poets sing about, except perhaps in a lachrymose way. It was not a prepossessing location, even though an electric utility later dubbed it "The Best Location in the Nation." It was not that in the beginning.

The Cuyahoga is a very old, very crooked river, and its meandering course into the lake was grassy and marshy. Silt choked the mouth of the river, and sand bars, at every turn and twist in its convoluted bed, made passage very difficult even for flat-bottomed boats.

The valley itself, on the basis of old descriptions, was an unpleasant place. Side pools of trapped water, turned stagnant, gave off a fetid smell. Snakes in uncommonly large numbers slithered about at the water's edge. And the slow movement of the bateaux through the still water stirred clouds of mosquitoes into furious action.

On either side of the river were high, heavily forested banks that cast heavy shadows on the water below and made the valley even less cheerful. But while the overall effect was sombre, the spirits of the founding party were high.

The point of debarkation, according to expert surmise, was apparently at the foot of Superior Street hill, just below Old River Road. That place has been designated as "Settlers Landing," and an appropriate marker identifies the place.

Among those who accompanied General Cleaveland ashore were his principal aides, Augustus Porter, surveyor, and Seth Pease, astronomer and surveyor; second and third in command, respectively.

Other surveyors in the party were Amos Spafford, John Milton Holley, Richard M. Stoddard, and Moses Warren, Jr. Joshua Stow was in charge of the commissary, and Theodore Shepard was the party's physician. A married couple accompanied the pioneer contingent, Job Phelps Stiles and his wife, Tabitha Cumi.

The first foundations of the city-to-be were laid by Cleaveland with his three principal aides, Porter, Pease, and Spafford, during the few months that followed the landing.

The topography of flatland on top of a bluff, with steep hillsides leading down to the river, was a problem, but the planners managed somehow to impose their New England ideas on the site. The really remarkable thing is that the town plan they devised during their brief stay turned out to have lasting qualities. It established a permanent community center, fixing the pattern of the central city's development so firmly that the outline of today's downtown Cleveland is clearly visible in the rude drawing of the original plan.

All things considered, the brief beginning was an impressive one. Much had been accomplished in the less than five months since the Connecticut party under General Cleaveland had set out for the Western Reserve the previous June.

On October 18, 1796, General Cleaveland and his surveyors packed up their gear, loaded their boats, and took leave of the lonely townsite on the chilly Cuyahoga River. They left behind them a caretaking colony of three persons: Job and Tabitha Stiles and one Joseph Landon.

Moses Cleaveland, it ought to be noted, never returned to the town he had founded and that bore his name. The call of his native Connecticut was much too strong, and Cleaveland, apparently, was not the kind of man to be pulled back to the wilderness town simply out of sentiment. If he had, he probably would have been surprised to find out how much of his home state he and his men had left behind on the Ohio wilderness.

Cleveland from 1796 to 1825

THE FOREST CLEARING called Cleveland expanded its perimeter slowly; so slowly, in fact, that its growth at times was imperceptible. There was no flood of settlers from Connecticut, or from anywhere else, that the land-company investors had hoped for originally. The colonists came singly, or in pairs, usually, and there were long intervals when none at all appeared.

The Cuyahoga Valley, which has been called the Flats as long as anybody can remember, early gained a fierce, repellent reputation among wanderers in the wilderness seeking a place to settle. The Flats, in its own way, was as bad a breeding place for malaria-bearing mosquitoes as the steamy jungles of Central America or the islands of the South Pacific.

The pioneer families could cope with the numerous rattlesnakes, but there was no way they could fight the invisible fever and win. The wise ones moved on. In midsummer of 1800, the field agent of the Connecticut Land Company, Turhand Kirtland, gloomily reported in a letter to Moses Cleaveland that the town named in his honor had only three inhabitants—all discontented. They were Major Spafford, Maj. Lorenzo Carter, and David Clark. Carter, who arrived in 1797, would be the first permanent white settler of the town.

Later, by 1810, things had picked up. Some fifty-seven persons called Cleveland their home, and a lot of historic firsts had been registered.

The first white child was born on January 23, 1797. Charles Phelps Stiles was the name given to the child, born to Job and Tabitha Stiles.

The first religious service also took place that year; a funeral service for a surveyor, David Eldridge, who drowned as he attempted to ford the Grand River on horseback on June 3, 1797, en route to Cleveland.

This tragic event led to the establishment of Cleveland's first cemetery, a plot on the east side of Ontario Street, north of Prospect Avenue. It was not far from a large Indian mound also on Ontario Street. There were a number of such prehistoric mounds in the vicinity of the hamlet.

THE WAY IT WAS in 1800 where the Cuyahoga flows into Lake Erie: The cabin on the extreme right housed the surveyors and was known as "Pease's Hotel." To its immediate left was the log warehouse for the party's supplies, while the third cabin, in the center of the drawing, was the cabin of the city's first permanent settler, Lorenzo Carter. The high mound on the east bank of the river was the creation of the ancient Mound Builder Indians. It was destroyed a few years after the village was founded when the river was cut through and widened. (CPL)

Cleveland's first wedding took place on July 4, 1797. In that ceremony, a domestic named Chloe Inches was joined to a man named William Clement. Their honeymoon took them away from the town permanently.

Among the most distinguished residents of Cleveland in its founding days was the famous Indian, Chief Seneca, who lived on the banks of the Cuyahoga until 1809. A less distinguished redskin was one named John O'Mick, who was the defendant in the first trial in town in 1812. Alfred Kelley, the town's first lawyer, served as prosecuting attorney. O'Mick was convicted of murder and was given the dubious distinction of being the first person to be executed in Cleveland. The hanging took place in Public Square on June 26, 1812, before the largest crowd ever to assemble in the remote wilderness outpost.

While Cleveland's population remained at a minimal level, a considerable number of people had moved inland, four miles to the southeast to Newburgh Township, located on a high ridge removed from the noxious vapors and mists and mosquitoes of the miasmic Cuyahoga Valley. James Kingsbury and his family, after testing the Cleveland climate briefly in 1797, were the first to make this move. By 1800, Newburgh had a population of ten families, while Cleveland's permanent population was down to one family—that of Major Carter.

In 1805, the Indians, by treaty, relinquished their title to the lands of the Connecticut Reserve west of the Cuyahoga River, thus opening up new territory to white settlement. The West Side's first settler was said to be John Haberton, who built a cabin on a high bank overlooking Rocky River, five miles west of Cleveland, in 1807. Cleveland's first black settler, George Peake, also selected to live on the West Side in 1809.

Enough settlers had spread about on the flat and fertile lands of the West Side by June 1, 1818, that it was incorporated as Brooklyn Township. Out of this large area later grew

Ohio City, West Cleveland, Brooklyn Village, Brighton or South Brooklyn, Linndale, Brooklyn Heights, and Lakewood.

The rivalry between Brooklyn and Cleveland on opposite banks of the river developed in intensity as the years passed, and especially as a new city with the grand name, the City of Ohio, grew out of Brooklyn. The two municipalities became one, in time, but the rivalry still continues.

Even though the population rise in Cleveland came slowly; it was an unusually busy town in its early days. The shipbuilding industry that was to prove such an important element in the town's growth, for example, got its first nudge in 1808 when Lorenzo Carter build a 45-ton boat, the *Zephyr*. Another boat-builder was Levi Johnson, a versatile carpenter who also built the log courthouse and jail on Public Square and the first frame house in town, for Judge Walworth.

Ships didn't have an easy time making their way into Cleveland's harbor because, until it was dredged and deepened in the late 1820s, the harbor was only about three feet deep. Not until 1818 was a lighthouse built and the first harbor lights were installed.

The most important man in the town's early history, by far, was Alfred Kelley, who was not only the first lawyer, but who also served as the village's first "president," after Cleveland was incorporated on December 23, 1814. Twelve residents cast ballots in the historic first election held in the village in June 1815.

Population growth increased considerably in the decade that followed, so that by 1825 Cleveland had a total of 500 residents—a marked improvement over the three persons who had called the town their home in 1800.

THE FIRST PERMANENT SETTLER in Cleveland was Maj. Lorenzo Carter, a tough, enterprising pioneer who operated the settlement's first tavern-hotel and who served as unofficial mayor, sheriff, and chief magistrate until the village government was formed in 1814. (CPL)

THE FIRST LIGHTHOUSE to guide boats into Cleveland harbor was built at the foot of Water Street (West Ninth) in 1818. In August of that year, the first steam-powered vessel on the Great Lakes, the famous *Walk-in-Water,* visited the little town. Sandbars blocked the entrance to the river in those days, however, and the best the 330-ton steamship could do was anchor quite a distance offshore and send its passengers in by rowboat. (Plain Dealer)

THE GREATEST of Cleveland's early citizens was Alfred Kelley, who moved to the Lake Erie village in 1810 from Oneida, New York, and quickly established himself as a standout member of the community. He was admitted to the bar the same year at the age of twenty-one, becoming one of the town's first lawyers. From 1814 to 1822 he represented Cuyahoga County in the Ohio Legislature. On December 23, 1814, he persuaded the legislature to grant Cleveland a charter of incorporation as a village. In the town's first election in June 1815, he was elected Cleveland's "president;" in effect, the first mayor. Kelley later was instrumental in getting Cleveland named as the northern terminal of the new Ohio-Erie Canal and, after that, headed the drive to provide the city with its first railroad. (CPL)

A PIONEER EDUCATOR was Harvey Rice, a graduate of Williams College, who decided to find his future in the western wilderness and journeyed to the Lake Erie hamlet that was Cleveland in September 1824. He blueprinted the city's educational system and helped to bring it into being as well as serving as one of the young community's leading civic spirits. Among other things, he was responsible for the Perry Monument that was placed on Public Square in 1860 and held the place of honor in that civic center until late 1892, when it was replaced by the Soldiers & Sailors Monument. (CPL)

Cleveland from 1825 to 1850

EVEN THOUGH a whole world of would-be settlers looked hungrily at maps that showed the empty interior of the North American continent, the migratory movement was nothing more than a trickle until the nineteenth century had passed its first quarter.

The trouble, of course, was transportation; or, more accurately, the lack of good transportation. Middle America was landlocked country. It was shut off from the populous East Coast by the formidable Appalachian Mountains running all the way from Canada down into Georgia. The main route of migratory movement was from Pittsburgh west, via the Ohio River. Not many travelers had the desire or reason to detour northward from the river route into the wilderness. A settlement like Cleveland on Lake Erie was too far out of the way.

But the situation changed in Cleveland's favor in 1825 when the Erie Canal in New York State had its grand opening. That man-made ditch, a 363-mile waterway joining the Hudson River with the Great Lakes, made it possible for the first time for millions of people to find their way into the heart of inland America.

Even before the Erie Canal began operation, Ohio had embarked on a program of building its own connections between Lake Erie and the Ohio River; not one canal, but two of them.

Cleveland, thanks to its strategic site on a natural water route into central and southern Ohio, was selected as the northern terminal of the 350-mile canal leading to Portsmouth on the Ohio River. The effect on Cleveland of the new canals—the one in New York State and the one in Ohio—was immediate and significant.

By autumn of 1825, some two thousand men were hard at work on the new Ohio-Erie Canal in the Cuyahoga Valley. And in the spring of the following year, the first tidal wave of human beings to be set in motion by the Erie Canal in New York pushed its way into the Northwest Territory.

Cleveland could count only 1,100 residents in 1831, the year the Ohio-Erie Canal opened. Two years later, in 1835, the population had jumped to 5,080. On the other side of the Cuyahoga River, Ohio City had 1,150 people.

ONE OF the city's earliest giants was Leonard Case, Sr., who became a resident in 1816, taking the post of cashier of the Commercial Bank of Lake Erie, just organized. He was a prominent lawyer, banker, and financier with a hand in virtually every civic development for nearly half a century. Upon his death in 1864, he left $1 million in property, the proceeds of which were used to establish the famous Case School of Applied Science, now part of Case-Western Reserve University. (CPL)

The Public Square still was the center of community life, but the residential district had pushed east as far as Muirson Street (East Twelfth Street). And the newly improved harbor and river facilities gave Cleveland the look of an important port.

A 600-foot pier had been built out into the lake in the late 1820s, and, thanks to federal dredging, ships at last were able to make their way into the river. The arrivals of nearly two thousand boats were recorded in 1835. Some seventy of these were from foreign ports, via the recently opened Welland Canal.

On May 8, 1836, the people of Cleveland celebrated a milestone event. On that day it became a city. The celebration probably would have been a lot more spirited if it had not

THE CONSTRUCTION of the Ohio-Erie Canal, begun in 1825 and completed in 1832, opened a new era of growth and development in Cleveland. Riding a canal boat was infinitely more comfortable than walking, riding a horse, or traveling by stage coach over rough corduroy roads and rutted dirt trails. More important, the canal provided an efficient means for the movement of produce and supplies through the primitive countryside and thick forests.

DAILY LINE OF OHIO CANAL PACKETS

Between Cleveland & Portsmouth.

DISTANCE 309 MILES--THROUGH IN 80 HOURS.

A Packet of this Line leaves Cleveland every day at 4 o'clock P. M. and Portsmouth every day at 9 o'clock A. M.

T. INGRAHAM, *Office foot of Superior-street, Cleveland,*
OTIS & CURTIS, *General Stage Office,* do. } AGENTS.
G. J. LEET, - - - - - *Portsmouth,*

NEIL, MOORE & CO.'S Line of Stages leaves Cleveland daily for Columbus, via Wooster and Hebron.
OTIS & CURTIS' Line of Stages leaves Cleveland daily for Pittsburgh, Buffalo, Detroit and Wellsville.

THE YEAR WAS 1833, and Cleveland was experiencing its first growing pains under the influence of its new Ohio-Erie Canal role. The view is from the corner of Bank (West Sixth Street) and St. Clair Avenue, looking east. The building with the spire on the left is the old Academy. The building in the center with the square tower is Trinity Church. To its right is the tower, featuring clocks, of the First Presbyterian Church, forerunner of the Old Stone Church. (CPL)

been that the rival town on the west side of the Cuyahoga had nosed out Cleveland for corporate honors five days earlier, on May 3, 1836. That community, at the same time, had assumed the impressive name, the City of Ohio.

The Cleveland-Ohio City rivalry, which reached the point of a small civil war during a bridge controversy in 1837, fizzled out as Cleveland gradually made the competition a runaway race. Ohio City lost its identity in 1854 when it was ignominiously annexed by Cleveland. The feeling of separateness, however, never has been completely eliminated. The West Side is still on the other side of the river, and the twain really have never met completely.

THE CLEVELAND GRAYS already were a part of the city's life in 1839 when an unknown artist put down on canvas this picture of the Cleveland military elite parading on Public Square. The location is the northwest corner of the Square. The first Old Stone Church is in the rear, center. (WRHS)

PUBLIC SQUARE, looking westward, as it was depicted by an artist in 1840: The white building in the center foreground is one of the town's first hotels, the Forest City House. It stands at the southwest corner of Superior Avenue and Public Square, a site that had been reserved for hotel use since the beginning of the city. The Sheraton-Cleveland Hotel has stood there since the early 1920s. (WRHS)

THE FIRST PIER from the foot of Water Street (West Ninth Street) was Stockly's Pier, built in 1849 by John G. Stockly. It extended 924 feet into the lake. Until then, explains the author of a footnote under the engraving, the downtown shore "was a continuous sand beach strewn with drift wood." (CPL)

[22]

THE FLATS before industry took over: The Cuyahoga Valley was a marine center when this sketch was drawn about 1842. Sailing ships and warehouses dominated the scene, but there still were homes and small farms. (WRHS)

Cleveland from 1850 to 1875

CLEVELAND WAS DESTINY'S CHILD in the second half of the nineteenth century. All the elements, all the signs, all the advantages that had led so many wise men to prophesy future greatness for Moses Cleaveland's town seemed to come together at last. The combination was powerful enough to turn visions into reality.

Small as the city was in 1850, it had begun to take on certain mature touches worthy of a city of 17,034. Large, elegant homes were springing up along lower Euclid Avenue, that the year before had been equipped with gaslights.

Progress could be seen also in the new curbside clutter of tall poles to carry wires for the telegraph, a marvelous improvement that had arrived in 1847. Among the major beneficiaries of the new facility, certainly, were the daily newspapers. There were three of them then, the *Plain Dealer,* the *Herald,* and the *Leader.*

A modern medical center, Marine Hospital, had been built on Lakeside Avenue, east of Erie (East Ninth), and a medical college had taken over the corner of Erie and St. Clair Avenue.

The First Presbyterian Church on the north side of the Square, built in 1832, was replaced by the congregation in 1853 with a more impressive edifice.

The new church, like its predecessor, was best known as the Old Stone Church. It still stands and it still carries that name; it is the last remaining link of the Public Square with its earliest years.

An imposing Federal Building was built on the east side of the Square, on the site of the Leonard Case home, between 1858-60. During that same period, a new, modern Court House replaced the primitive 1828 building on the north side of the Square. A third impressive addition to downtown was the five-story Case Block on Superior Avenue.

But Cleveland at mid-century, while busy and growing, was no more than a mercantile town; a port. There was the feeling that industry was needed if the city was to advance.

The age of the railroad was well underway, but Cleveland, unfortunately, had not kept pace in the race for rail service. In 1847, responding to the appeals of Clevelanders who knew his talent for action, the legendary Alfred Kelley, by that time a citizen of Columbus, came to Cleveland's aid once again.

Kelley became the organizer, builder, and the president of a railroad long in the planning stage, the Cleveland, Columbus and Cincinnati Railroad, moving on the project with such dispatch that the line was completed and had trains in operation between Cleveland and Columbus by February 18, 1851.

This improvement in the city's transportation facilities was basic in the rapid industrialization that followed. But other important steps had been taken.

Two Cleveland-financed companies, the Cleveland Iron Company and the Dead River & Ohio Mining Company, had launched explorations of mineral deposits in Michigan's Upper Peninsula and around Lake Superior in the 1840s.

The Cleveland Iron Mining Company, an outgrowth of Cleveland Iron Company, began business in 1853 and gave Cleveland investors their initial foothold in the Lake Superior mining country. Those investors, in the first ten years, took millions of dollars worth of copper and silver ore from the rich deposits of the Upper Peninsula.

The notion that Cleveland could be developed into a giant iron center fascinated a number of imaginative businessmen. They saw the city as a logical meeting place for the coal of Southern Ohio and West Virginia and the iron ore of the North. By the 1860s, the junction of the minerals successfully effected, the skies above the Cleveland Flats were red from the reflected glare of iron-making plants.

A corollary development was the spread of Cleveland influence in lake shipping, a natural outgrowth of the need to move ore by way of the lakes to the Cleveland mills. The iron companies poured money into lake carriers.

Within the ten-year period from 1850 to 1860, the city's population grew two and one-half times, shooting upward from 17,034 to 43,417. The countywide population, meanwhile, rose to 78,000.

More significant, perhaps, than the rise in the population was the change in its character. Immigration in previous decades had been largely of native New England stock. By 1860, more than forty-four percent of the people living in Cleveland were of foreign origin, and the New Englanders had become a minority. Cleveland suddenly had become a cosmopolitan city of Germans, English, Irish, Scotch, Welsh, Czechs, Hungarians, and Italians.

Railroad tracks, criss-crossing the city by the 1860s, had preempted the choice land along the lakefront and the riverfront, usurping scenic areas that rightly should have been reserved for recreational use. But people didn't mind too much the loss then. There was nothing more beautiful to the eyes of most Americans in that time than tall factory stacks pouring out black smoke.

There was a brighter side. The main streets, hitherto muddy and rutted, were paved. Superior Avenue, for example, was given a foundation of stone and planks, then coated with sand, in 1850. Euclid Avenue was just beginning its golden age, with new homes of magnificent proportions rising along the way as far east as the city limits at Willson Avenue (East Fifty-fifth Street). They created a sight so imposing that a famous lecturer

"A PROSPECT VARIED AND BEAUTIFUL" is the way a magazine, *Gleason's Pictorial Drawing Room Companion,* described Cleveland harbor in 1852, the date of this sketch. "Like all our western cities," said the magazine, "it is hourly increasing in wealth and the number of its population and bids fair to be, in time, a second Cincinnati."

A PANORAMIC VIEW OF THE CITY, looking east over the Cuyahoga River Valley, as it appeared in 1853: The wide street in the center is Superior Avenue. There was still farmland in the Flats downtown. (CPL)

of the day, John Fiske, speaking before the Royal Society of Great Britain in 1860, said the vista reminded him "of the nave and aisles of a huge cathedral."

Not for nothing was Cleveland coming to be known nationally as the "Forest City." Urbanization had hardly made a dent in the thick groves of trees that grew along the lakeshore. They were banked together in such profusion that only the highest church spires could pierce the leafy overhang. Not surprisingly, when the city's first baseball team took the field in 1865, it bore the name, the Forest City Club.

An imposing monument to Commodore Oliver Hazard Perry and a central fountain had given the Public Square a park-like appearance until 1867, when pressure from the merchants forced the city to allow two avenues, Superior and Ontario, to bisect the city center. That fragmentation ruined its character beyond repair.

Perhaps the most important happening in Cleveland's eventful first century was the arrival in town in 1853 of a family from New York, headed by a traveling salesman named William Avery Rockefeller. One of his three sons was a fourteen-year-old named John D. Rockefeller who would make his mark in Cleveland very quickly and lay the groundwork for an oil empire, with Cleveland the control center in the beginning years at least.

In 1863, when he was only twenty-two years old, Rockefeller organized a refining company called Andrews, Clark & Company, which, by the close of the Civil War, was one of thirty oil refineries in Cleveland. Rockefeller consolidated all of them into one great company. In January 1870, he founded the Standard Oil Company.

The Oil King had to take up residence in New York City in 1882 to properly manage his global business affairs, but his heart was back home in Cleveland. He returned to his Forest Hill estate every summer until 1918.

Lakeview Cemetery in Cleveland is the final resting place of the Rockefellers. A tall memorial shaft marks the family plot. Streets and parks and buildings still bear the Rockefeller name. What is not visible in Cleveland is the strength that Rockefeller imparted to the city while it was in its adolescent stage.

[26]

CENTRAL HIGH SCHOOL in 1856 had as one of its students John D. Rockefeller. The school was at the corner of Erie (East Ninth) and Euclid. (News)

BELIEVED TO BE the oldest photograph of Public Square, this picture, taken in 1857, looks east on Superior Avenue towards the shady park that once decorated the center of the city. Superior Avenue and Ontario Street were blocked by a rail fence that surrounded the Square, whose feature attraction was an elegant fountain erected for the State Fair held in Cleveland in 1856. It was in that year the city first began pumping its drinking water out of Lake Erie, and thousands of Clevelanders got their first taste of later water by scooping it up out of the fountain base. (News)

[27]

CUYAHOGA COUNTY'S second courthouse, on the southwest corner of Public Square, is seen in its last days about 1858. Demolition of the old building, constructed in 1826, already appears to be underway. The dome is shredded, bricks have been toppled, and the lower part of the building is plastered with posters. (WRHS)

THE FAMILIAR "Watch Us Grow" slogan had not been put up at the site in 1860, but this is where the May Company now stands on Euclid Avenue, facing the Public Square. The handsome house shown in this remarkably sharp old photograph belonged to Richard Winslow and his family. (Plain Dealer)

[28]

THE GLORY DAYS came early for the Weddell House, Cleveland's most famous hotel in the last half of the nineteenth century. President Lincoln chose the balcony of the hotel as the place from which to speak to the people of the city in 1861 on the way to his inauguration in Washington. The sketch by an unknown artist looks west towards the hotel at the corner of Superior and Bank Street (West Sixth Street). (Plain Dealer)

THE MIDDLE INITIAL in John D. Rockefeller's name could have stood for the determination so plain on his face in the photograph at right, taken when he was only twenty years old late in 1859. He already had made his mark as a successful commission merchant engaged in the buying and selling of grain, pork, and other farm products, working out of an office on Merwin Street in the Flats. Rockefeller's first venture into the oil business was under the banner of Rockefeller & Andrews, a partnership that had its offices in this building *(above)* at the intersection of Merwin Street and Superior Avenue in the Flats. A scene about 1865, the Cuyahoga River is in the right background. (Murway-Sohio)

A PAVILION was hastily erected on Public Square to receive the body of Abraham Lincoln following his assassination in 1865. The funeral coach, drawn by six white horses, is shown backed up to the catafalque. More than one hundred thousand persons paid their respects to the martyred President during the day and into the night. Looking directly ahead, beyond the pavilion is the view east on Superior Avenue. The monument to the left is the memorial to Commodore Oliver Hazard Perry. (News)

THE UNION PASSENGER STATION at the foot of Water (West Ninth) and Bank (West Sixth) streets, along the lakefront, as it looked not long after it was opened in November 1866. It was a stone building some 603 feet long and 108 feet wide, and generally considered to be a rather grand structure. By the time the Van Sweringens built the new Union Terminal on Public Square, however, the old station had become a civic disgrace. (CPL)

THE SOLDIERS' AID SOCIETY was an important agency in 1865 when hundreds of returning veterans sought help in rejoining the ranks of employed civilians. The two men, center, standing on either side of the barrel were likely among the veterans. It will be noticed that the man on the left is minus a leg. The office was at 95 Bank Street (West Sixth), which was a bit on the muddy side that day. (WRHS)

THE TEST DEMONSTRATION of a fire hose from the city's first fire engine in 1869 drew a big crowd to Public Square. The view is looking east. The Forest City House on the site of today's Hotel Sheraton-Cleveland is to the right. (Plain Dealer)

THE SILVERTHORN INN, shown here probably in the 1870s, stood on the site of the Westlake Hotel in Rocky River. (WRHS)

THE OLD MAIN LIGHT that stood at the entrance to Cleveland harbor at the middle of the nineteenth century was atop a handsome tower. Next to it was the dwelling of the lighthouse keeper. The two were at the foot of Water Street (West Ninth) close to the mouth of the Cuyahoga River. (News)

MEMBERS of the Cleveland Grays Band, sagging under the weight of their epaulets, took time out from their tootling to pose for this group photo in 1872. (Plain Dealer)

ONE OF THE MOST IMPRESSIVE of Cleveland's early churches was the Second Presbyterian Church shown here as it looked in 1870. It stood on the site of today's Cuyahoga Building, on Superior Avenue, adjacent to Public Square. The beautiful stone edifice was built in 1850 and destroyed by fire in 1876. (CPL)

A SO-CALLED DUMMY RAILROAD, the steam-driven trains of the Newburgh & Kinsman Line, provided service between Cleveland and Newburgh. One of the trains is shown in 1870 as it crossed the wooden bridge over Kinsbury Run.

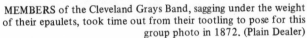

THE END of the Franco-Prussian War was the signal for the Cleveland German community to celebrate, and they whooped it up in grand style with this Arch of Triumph—Triumpfbogen—erected over
Superior Avenue on Public Square. A three-day "Peace Jubilee" in April 1871, ended with a parade
two miles long passing under the arch. The Perry Monument is to the right. (Ambrose)

LEISURELY PROMENADING in 1872 was pursued on the Reservoir Walk around the city reservoir
that covered a large acreage from Franklin and Kentucky (West Thirty-eighth Street) avenues south to
Woodbine Avenue. The view here is to the north, overlooking Franklin. A Methodist church is in the
foreground, at the corner of Franklin and today's West Thirty-second Street. In the distance, directly
behind the rear of the Methodist church is the spire of Saint John's Episcopal Church, while the steeple in the center probably belongs to Saint Malachi's Catholic Church atop the old Angle. (CPL)

DOWNTOWN'S BUILDINGS hadn't grown tall enough
in 1872 to crowd out the view of Lake Erie to the northwest. The foreground shows the north side of Superior
Avenue at Seneca Street (West Third). To the upper
right is a building occupied by *The Plain Dealer* on
Seneca Street and Frankfort. (CPL)

THE OLD STONE CHURCH on Public Square is seen in
1875 from the south-side site of the present-day Higbee
Company: The beloved lily fountain is in the foreground.
The steeple of the Old Stone Church later was destroyed
by fire. At the extreme right of the picture the Critten-
den Home stands where later on the Society for Savings
Building was built. (CPL)

THE CUYAHOGA VALLEY already lay under a pall of
smoke from industry by 1875, and sailing ships from all
over jammed the available docking facilities in the river
and the harbor. (Plain Dealer)

[34]

Cleveland from 1875 to 1900

CLEVELAND PASSED the century's three-quarter mark like a runaway locomotive on a steep grade, in much too much of a hurry to pause for the ceremonial amenities. It was on a big trip under a full head of steam, headed for bigger things.

It seemed as if all roads led to the city in that giddy time of growth. By 1880 the official count showed 160,146 people in residence, making Cleveland the nation's twelfth largest city—a big jump over the 92,829 in the census of 1870, when Cleveland ranked fifteenth.

But the people boom was just getting underway. The 1890 census revealed a population of 261,353; a gain of more than 100,000 in a mere ten years. And it made Cleveland the tenth largest city in the United States.

As the 1880s came to a close, Cleveland was being served by eleven railroads, and the Ohio-Erie Canal, the miracle of the century's middle years, already was being phased out of service. It had become obsolete after only sixty years.

During the 1880s, the number of manufacturing concerns had grown to 2,300 and the number of products manufactured had doubled, as had their value. There were three times as many people on the payrolls, three times as much capital invested by manufacturers.

Industry had reached out eastward as far as Doan Street (East One-hundred and seventh) and as far west as Gordon Street (West Sixty-fifth).

The city administration, which had lived in rented quarters in the Jones Building on Superior Avenue from 1855 to 1874, moved into the big Case Block on Superior in 1875. The Federal Building and Post Office took over the site later.

In 1894 the voters authorized construction of a City Hall. Mayor McKisson chose the northern half of Public Square as the best, most economical site. The area shortly was enclosed by a board fence and excavation was begun after the groundbreaking ceremony on June 4, 1895.

The immediate public outcry over the spoiling of Public Square was so loud and so sustained, though, that the city administration reconsidered its plan of action. The diggers stopped digging and refilled the hole, the fences came down, and the new City Hall died aborning. The people had decided that the destruction of Public Square was too much of a price to pay.

On that same Square, a few years earlier, there had been the demonstration of a miracle that shortly had global repercussions. There, on April 29, 1879, Charles F. Brush, one of Cleveland's brightest scientists, exhibited the world's first electrical street light. A number of 150-foot high poles were set about the Square, each equipped with twelve arc-light lamps.

At 8:05 that night, while thousands of people crowded nervously about the Square, the switch was turned on and the lights glowed. Within six months, the city contracted for Brush arc lights to be installed on the Square and several city streets, giving Cleveland the distinction of becoming the first community in the world to light its streets with electricity. Then, to cinch the city's claim as an electrical innovator, the world's first electric streetcar was demonstrated on Public Square in that same year, 1879, and regular service by the new type of vehicle began in Cleveland before the year was up.

Not all of the events that took place on Public Square during those hectic decades of the late nineteenth century were happy ones. The bodies of two martyr-Presidents rested on display in the city's center within the incredibly short period of sixteen years: Abraham Lincoln in 1865 and James A. Garfield in 1881.

Nine years after Clevelanders had paid their respects to President Garfield, a massive mausoleum-monument to hold his remains was dedicated in Lakeview Cemetery as a national shrine. It was built at a cost of $225,000, financed by contributions from school children of all forty-eight states.

Cleveland had many things to celebrate as the Gay Nineties rounded out its century of incomparable success, and these were all wrapped up in one grand outburst of civic pride and thanksgiving, which was reserved for the most appropriate year of all, 1896—the year of the city's 100th birthday.

In its one hundred years, Cleveland had advanced from a forested site on Lake Erie known only to Indians, trappers, and wild animals to a city inhabited by a quarter-million people. It had become a large industrial center that was the tenth-largest city in the United States.

There was a lot to celebrate, obviously, and the citizens were determined to mark the big birthday properly.

A log cabin was built on the northeast quadrant of Public Square, but the main adornment of the city center was a mighty arch, similar to the Arc de Triomphe in Paris, that straddled Superior Avenue near Ontario Street. It was a magnificent creation, overpowering in its size and majesty, and it symbolized as nothing else could the bursting pride of the people in their city's growth and achievements.

The big moment that focused all the pride and enthusiasm of the century arrived at 8:15 p.m. on the evening of Founders Day, July 22, 1896. A solid mass of people filled

MID-AFTERNOON TRAFFIC moved along the cobblestones of
Superior Avenue West on this sunny day in 1875, mainly open
carriages and horse-drawn streetcars. The view is east towards the
Public Square. The Forest City House is the farthest building on
the right, where the Square begins. (Baus)

WHEN CLEVELAND was at its picturesque best downtown, in
the period around 1875, this is the way the city's lighthouse
looked. It was at the intersection of Main Street and Water Street
(West Ninth Street). (Baus)

THE BEST HOTEL IN TOWN for many years was the Forest City
House, shown here in 1875. The view is from the sidewalk on the
south side of Public Square, in front of what today is the Higbee
Company store. (Baus)

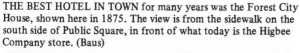

[37]

the Square at that time for the ceremonial opening of the official celebration as symbolized by the lighting for the first time of the Centennial Arch.

It was to be no ordinary switching-on of the lights. No less a man than the President of the United States, Grover Cleveland, himself a relative of old Moses Cleaveland, had agreed to perform the honors. At precisely 8:15 that night, he pushed a button in his summer home at Buzzard's Bay, Massachusetts, magically causing the lights of the arch in Cleveland to burst out in all their brilliance.

It was a big, beautiful moment; perhaps the grandest moment of a century that had been more successful than the old Connecticut Yankees ever would have dared to dream.

THE AMERICAN CENTENNIAL was celebrated on Public Square in Cleveland on July 4, 1876, with this thrilling free balloon ascension, the first aeronautical exhibition in the city's history. (Plain Dealer)

A HOTEL HAS STOOD at the southwest corner of Public Square and Superior Avenue since Cleveland was a hamlet in 1815. Mowrey's Tavern, the first on the site, had its name changed later to the Cleveland House. It burned down in 1845, but three years later the Dunham House was built, and was renamed the Forest City House in 1852. It is shown as it looked in 1876. (News)

FOREST HILL, the residence of the Rockefeller family, was in East Cleveland. The house originally was used as a hospital and served briefly as a hotel before it became the home of the Oil King and his family about 1878. (Plain Dealer)

CRUDE OIL was shipped in these primitive railroad tank cars when the oil industry was in its early days in Cleveland. They were simply flat cars carrying two round wooden vats holding a total of about 1,700 gallons of oil. (Sohio)

WHEN THE SUPERIOR VIADUCT over the Cuyahoga Valley and the busy industrial river was completed and dedicated on December 27, 1878, it was hailed as an engineering masterpiece. It measured 3,211 feet in length, connecting the West Side with downtown Cleveland. A draw span in the middle was 332 feet long and stood 68 feet above the river. Tall masted freighters required that the draw span pivot sideways to allow them passage. Cost of the viaduct, the principal traffic thoroughfare over the valley until 1916, was $2,150,000. An 1885 photograph shows a view from the center draw of the viaduct looking westward. The tower of old Saint Malachi's Church is visible to the far left. Note the wooden sidewalks and the horse-drawn streetcar whose conductor is patiently waiting for the photographer. The west arches of the angled viaduct seen in this picture still stand. (Plain Dealer)

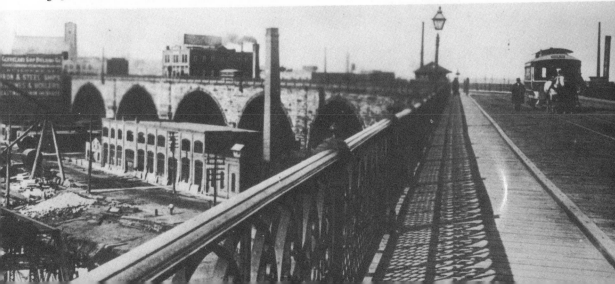

BIRTH OF A MODERN MIRACLE: As thousands of Clevelanders and city visitors looked on in awe, the world's first outdoor demonstration of the electric arc light took place on Public Square on April 29, 1879. This is an artist's conception of the dramatic event. Charles F. Brush of Cleveland was the inventor of the arc light; two years later, he was one of the founders of the Cleveland Electric Illumination Company. (CEIC)

THE MOST SPECTACULAR EVIDENCE that Charles F. Brush was a scientist and inventor was this huge windmill that stood behind his Euclid Avenue mansion in the late nineteenth century. Brush designed it and built it as part of his experimentation in the generation of electrical power. (WRHS)

THE BARN of the Superior Railway Company, shown here in 1880, was at the end of the line at Wilson Street (East Fifty-fifth Street) and Superior Avenue. The vehicle on the tracks on the right was one of the "summer" cars which carried forty passengers and required two horses to pull it. The fare was five cents in the daytime, ten cents at night. (Reeves)

THE WEDDELL HOUSE was not quite so elegant by the latter part of the nineteenth century (probably the 1880s). The main part of the building had to give way to the Rockefeller Building just after the turn of the century. (Plain Dealer)

ANDREWS' FOLLY was the name Clevelanders gave this elaborate Victorian dreadful that was built at the corner of Euclid Avenue and Sterling Street (East Thirtieth Street) by Samuel Andrews, one of John D. Rockefeller's early partners. The mansion, built about 1882, contained thirty-three rooms, including five separate suites for each of the millionaire's five daughters. It is said that the English-born Andrews hoped to entertain Queen Victoria herself in the house, but if she received the invitation, she never responded to it. The Andrews family occupied the house only three years. One of the major household problems was that it required a staff of 100 servants to maintain domestic harmony. The old house stood unoccupied until it was torn down in 1937. A television station, WEWS, later took over the site. (Plain Dealer)

MOUSTACHES AND WHISKERS were the order of the day when this picture was taken sometime late in the nineteenth century. The subjects were the policemen of the third precinct. Only two of them are clean-shaven. (City)

JEPTHA H. WADE, a self-made man, was one of many success stories in Cleveland during the middle years of the nineteenth century. His principal business achievement was putting together the nationally important Western Union Telegraph Company. Upon his death in 1882, he bequeathed a large, forested tract of land to the city for public use, Wade Park, reserving four acres for some civic use to be determined later. His grandson, also named Jeptha H. Wade, specified that the four acres should be the site of the future Cleveland Art Museum. (CPL)

THE STILLMAN HOTEL opened in 1884, was a fine-looking edifice and one of the first commercial invaders of Euclid Avenue east of Erie Street (East Ninth Street), but it had a short-lived existence. The building was damaged by a serious fire in 1900 and its owner razed the building in 1901. The location was later used for the Stillman Theater. (News)

EUCLID AVENUE'S "Millionaires' Row" numbered these grand old mansions in its exclusive company before the turn of the century. The Sylvester Everett home *(above)* stood behind an iron picket fence at Case Street (East Fortieth Street) and Euclid Avenue. The William Chisholm mansion *(upper left)* was used for some years by the Cleveland Institute of Music. Streetcar magnate Tom L. Johnson, later to be the city's mayor, built the outstanding residence at Euclid and East Twenty-fourth Street *(below)*, while John Hay, the famous nineteenth century author and U.S. secretary of state, called this his Cleveland home *(lower left)* in 1881. (Plain Dealer)

[43]

THE OLDEST CHURCH in Cleveland, Saint John's Episcopal Church at the corner of Church Avenue and West Twenty-sixth Street, was virtually the same in appearance in 1888 as it is today. Even the little house to the right still stands in the old Ohio City neighborhood. (CPL)

[44]

FIREFIGHTING WAS A HERO'S GAME in the old days when this photograph of the Cleveland Veterans Volunteer Brigade was taken. The date is thought to be sometime in the 1880s. (CFD)

THE ROOFTOP EQUIPMENT shown around 1880 on top of the Kelley Block, the third building on the right, had nothing to do with air conditioning. The main exchange of the Bell Telephone Company was in this building on the south side of West Superior, opposite Bank Street (West Sixth Street), and the rooftop installation was part of the telephone equipment. The first telephone was installed in Cleveland in 1879. *The Cleveland Leader* occupied the building on the far right. (News)

[45]

THE SOCIETY FOR SAVINGS BUILDING was under construction when this picture was taken, probably in 1890. The old Court House, at extreme left, was still intact and the Old Stone Church, center, still carried a tall steeple. The dark shaft in the middle of the Square carried a cluster of electric lights at its top, but the idea proved impractical as a method of outdoor illumination. (Ambrose)

LONG BEFORE HE BECAME MAYOR, Tom L. Johnson took part in 1889 in a Charles Dickens costume party. Johnson, on the right, is shown with W. B. Hale in their portrayal of the Dickens characters called the Cheeryble Brothers. (Plain Dealer)

A CREW LAYING PIPELINES for gas paused in its labors long enough to pose for the photographer sometime in the 1890s. Derbies apparently were de rigueur in those days for gas-pipe gangs. (EOG)

ROCKEFELLER'S Standard Oil empire began here in the grimy upper reaches of the Flats in the Cuyahoga Valley. This is the first refinery of the global company, Standard Oil No. 1, in 1890. (Sohio)

AIR CONDITIONING was a standard feature of the early electric streetcars, as this 1890 photo of a Scranton Avenue speedster illustrates. (CTS)

TROLLEY HISTORY was being made on March 23, 1890, at the intersection of Erie Street (East Ninth) and Prospect and Huron. The picture, looking east towards the triangle, shows the first streetcar pulling a trailer. Electric-powered streetcars were only six years old at the time, and horse-drawn cars had not yet been fully phased out of operation. An interesting detail is the electric light-and-telephone pole bending under the weight of eleven crossarms. (Baus)

HOLD THE PRESSES! A couple of journalists are shown here in the glamorous editorial-room setting of The *Plain Dealer* before the turn of the century. Reporters dressed modishly even then. (Plain Dealer)

[48]

A GROUP OF SPORTING BLOODS paused in their larking about the links of the Country Club, circa 1890, to pose for this picture. Those who are identifiable are, standing left to right, L. Dean Holden, an unknown, Will Boardman, and Roy York. Sitting left to right, are Ben Crowell, Robert H. York, an unknown, and Kenyon Painter. (CPL)

TRAFFIC CAME TO A STANDSTILL when the photographer set up this picture of the old U. S. Post Office that stood at the corner of Superior Avenue and Public Square (site of the present Federal Building and Post Office) from 1858 to 1902. The scene, snapped in 1890, is made more interesting by the fact that the man in the foreground is holding a raccoon in his arms. That's still a standout stunt among people who want to win attention from photographers. (Plain Dealer)

COMMODORE OLIVER HAZARD PERRY beat the British in the War of 1812, but he lost the "Battle of Public Square" in Cleveland. His monument occupied this strategic southeast quadrant of Public Square from September 10, 1860, the forty-seventh anniversary of the Battle of Lake Erie, until December 3, 1892, when it was evicted to make way for the Soldiers and Sailors Monument. It ended up eventually in Gordon Park. Here's the way it appeared about 1885. The view is east, looking down Euclid Avenue. (Baus)

THE BRONZE STATUARY for the Soldiers and Sailors Monument was cast in a studio-barn behind the site of the Schofield Building at Erie Street (East Ninth) and Euclid Avenue, then occupied by a house. This photo was taken probably in 1893, the year before the completion of the monument. Louis Maroni, in charge of the casting process, is in the center of those in the left background. The hatted, white-gowned man seated in the foreground is Levi T. Schofield, designer of the famous monument. (Plain Dealer)

AFTER THE PARADE celebrating the dedication of the Soldiers and Sailors Monument on Public Square on July 4, 1894, the crowd of spectators swarmed all over the new city landmark. The traffic jam on Superior Avenue is worthy of any modern freeway. The view is towards the southwest. Total cost of the monument was $280,000. (Ambrose)

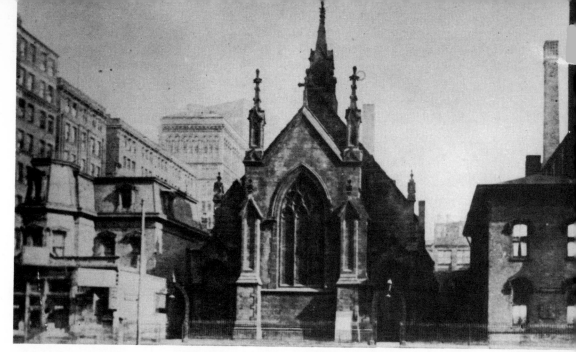

THE FIRST TRINITY EPISCOPAL CATHEDRAL stood in 1895 on Superior Avenue near East Sixth Street where the Leader Building now stands. To the right is the parish house. East of the church, behind the one-story commercial store, is the former home of Samuel Raymond. (CPL)

IN 1895, STREETCARS had to turn off Euclid Avenue at Erie Street (East Ninth) and travel on Prospect Avenue all the way to Case Avenue (East Fortieth Street) before they could return to Euclid. The detour was directly attributable to the distaste the residents of Millionaires' Row, between Erie and Case streets, felt for the noisy streetcars and the damage they might cause to the splendid avenue. The imposing edifice at the southwest corner of Erie and Euclid was the First Methodist Church. It was replaced later by the Cleveland Trust Company Bank building. (CPL)

SEVENTEEN PEOPLE DIED when, on the night of November 16, 1895, a streetcar speeding over the rails on the Central Viaduct plunged through the bridge's open draw into the Cuyahoga River. The bridge was lined with spectators the next morning as equipment grappled for the sunken streetcar below. (Plain Dealer)

THE DOWNTOWN LAKEFRONT looked quite different from today late in the nineteenth century— the Lakeside Hospitals were still in their original locations on Lakeside Avenue between East Twelfth and East Ninth streets, but Lake Erie lapped the base of the railroad tracks. Filling in of the lakefront had not yet started. It was to add hundreds of acres of land for the municipal parking lot, the Memorial Shoreway, and Burke Lakefront Airport. (WRHS)

PUBLIC UTILITIES operated on a modest, if not primitive level in their earlier days. The Cleveland Gas & Coke Company, whose wagon is shown here circa 1895—probably on East Ninth Street, in front of Saint John's Cathedral—was the predecessor of the East Ohio Gas Company. (EOG)

THE FAMOUS OLD ARCADE was quite new in June 1895, when two thousand delegates to the National Convention of Republicans Clubs took over the showplace of the Midwest for their banquet. The Arcade, designed by John M. Eisenmann and George H. Smith in the Romanesque Revival style of Victorian architecture, was built in 1890. Its five-story-high galleries connect two ten-story buildings, one on Euclid Avenue and the other on Superior Avenue. The historical landmark structure has been compared with the famed Galleria Vittorio Emmanuele in Milan, Italy. (Plain Dealer)

[53]

THE CITY HALL THAT NEVER WAS: Excavation in Public Square was begun for the construction of the new City Hall depicted in this artist's sketch, but the citizens in 1895 rebelled at the desecration of the park-like Public Square, and caused the city administration to cancel the project. It never was built. (Plain Dealer)

CLEVELAND'S CENTENNIAL CELEBRATION in 1896 was highlighted by the construction of a remarkable arch that straddled Superior Avenue on Public Square. (Plain Dealer)

Cleveland from 1900 to 1925

CLEVELAND'S RUSH towards maturity and greatness was not perceptibly slowed by the turn of the century. It roared out of the nineteenth century and into the dazzling light of the twentieth at top speed. The census count in 1900 gave Cleveland 381,768 persons, lifting it to the rank of seventh city. Cuyahoga County, in the same milestone year, was credited with 439,120 population.

On other counts, Cleveland found it had become an industrial giant—a center for the production of iron and steel; chemicals; paints, and varnishes; machine tools; boats; wagons; electrical products; bicycles; sewing machines; and ready-to-wear clothing. Coal, iron ore, and oil were the important ingredients in its economy, as were the railroads that brought them together.

In addition to all this, a new element began to take its place in the industrial potpourri; the machine called the automobile. A bicycle-maker named Alexander Winton had startled Clevelanders in 1896 when he rolled up and down the streets in a four-wheel gas buggy of his own creation. He became the city's first automobile manufacturer, and one of the first in the world.

Other enterprising Cleveland companies soon joined Winton in the production of autos, and the city, until 1904, was the world's leading manufacturer of motor cars. It remained an important center until 1932. During those three decades Cleveland produced some eighty different makes of cars!

There were more than nuts and bolts and smoking factory stacks in the scene, though. Cleveland also had become an important center of national political power by 1900. The personification of that power was Sen. Marcus Alonzo Hanna, mentor and manager of the political career of Pres. William F. McKinley. The latter's success made Cleveland a base of political power.

While Mark Hanna's death in 1904 deprived the city of one of its all-time political greats, another notable named Tom L. Johnson had risen to national heights as congressman and then mayor of the city. Johnson, a millionaire streetcar entrepreneur, became mayor in 1901 and held the office for eight years.

It was Mayor Johnson who initiated the reconstruction of the city's downtown through the so-called Group Plan, which included a new federal building, the Court House, a central mall, the Public Library, City Hall, the Public Auditorium, the underground Exposition Hall, and the Board of Education Building. Nearly $40 million was spent altogether. This great complex of classical public buildings gave Cleveland, for the first time, the look of a major city.

Construction of the Group Plan was still underway when a pair of brothers, O. P. and M. J. Van Sweringen, asserted themselves in Cleveland history. They gave the city a new suburb, built from scratch, and a new skyline.

The Van Sweringens, originally bicycle-shop operators, acquired 1,400 acres southeast of Cleveland and built Shaker Heights. To acquire right-of-way for a rapid transit line linking Shaker to downtown Cleveland, they bought a network of railroads and then built a new Union Terminal on Public Square to serve the rapid transit and the railroads alike. Their Terminal Tower and surrounding buildings, constructed between 1919 and 1930, cost $200 million. And the Tower, which stands atop the Union Terminal, rearing fifty-two stories up and 708 feet in height, was at that time the tallest building in the world outside of New York City.

During this period of physical growth, Clevelanders still held on to the political idealism of Tom L. Johnson, as they proved in January 1924, when they adopted a city manager form of government, a business-like style of city administration. It was an era that worshipped big business, and the city unquestionably had become a big business itself.

In 1910, Cleveland became sixth largest city in the United States with 560,663 population, an increase in ten years of 46.9%. In 1920, the count had reached 796,841, a forty-two per cent gain, making it the nation's fifth largest city.

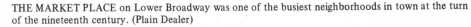

THE MARKET PLACE on Lower Broadway was one of the busiest neighborhoods in town at the turn of the nineteenth century. (Plain Dealer)

CLEVELAND'S WHITE SEWING MACHINE Company boosted the home city in its advertisements, as this ad wrapped around a photo of John D. Rockefeller's Forest Hill estate entrance shows. (White)

ONE OF THE EARLY ADVERTISEMENTS in which the White Sewing Machine Company touted the merits of the White Steam Car. (White)

There were radical physical changes in the mushrooming city. The residential neighborhoods downtown had given way to office buildings by 1915, and even Euclid Avenue, that boulevard of mansions, had become an avenue of memories and derelict houses. The wealthy families had evacuated in the face of creeping commercialism, fleeing to newly fashionable neighborhoods like Bratenahl on Lake Erie, Shaker Heights, Gates Mills, Cleveland Heights, East Cleveland, Lakewood, and Rocky River.

The shadows of the tall buildings darkened the wide downtown streets, but the city's future, nevertheless, never looked brighter than when the Turbulent Twenties reached their peak in 1925.

AMONG THE EARLIEST production automobiles in the United States was the famous White Stanhope Steamer, of which the first assembly line in 1901 is shown here. It was on the third floor of the White Sewing Machine Company on Canal Street in the Flats. The man on the extreme right was the production foreman. R. J. Schmunk. (White)

WHOA, AUTO!

Twelve Miles an Hour is a Fast Enough Gait.

Ordinance Regulating the Running of Horseless Vehicles—An Auto Club Formed.

The Cleveland Automobile club was formed, Monday evening, at a meeting of a dozen automobilists at the Chamber of Commerce. These officers were elected: E. L. Strong, president; Geo. Weiss, vice president; Windsor T. White, treasurer, and L. H. Rogers, secretary. General standing committees were appointed. An effort will be made to regulate the speed of autos in such a way that the public will be protected and the rights of the members preserved.

Councilman J. L. Reilly introduced an ordinance in the council, Monday night, to regulate automobiles. They must carry two lamps at night and a bell, which must be sounded during the day or night, when 100 feet away from street crossings. Speed is limited to 12 miles an hour. The ordinance provides a penalty of not more than $50 for violations thereof.

THE CLEVELAND AUTOMOBILE CLUB, the oldest existing association of its kind in the nation, got off to a fast, tire-screeching start on January 8, 1900, hardly waiting for the Century of the Automobile to begin. The news story in that day's *Cleveland Plain Dealer* announcing the organization of the club is shown along with news of a legislative proposal which would have required motorists to carry two lamps at night "and a bell, which must be sounded during the day or night, when 100 feet away from a street crossing." (Plain Dealer)

IRISH EYES WERE SMILING when a photographer took this picture of Ernest Roland Ball and his wife, Maud, as he rippled through a few of his tunes at the family piano. Ball, a native of Cleveland, was a talented pianist who became a song plugger in a downtown dime store at the turn of the century before going on to national fame as a composer and vaudeville performer. Among the four hundred songs he wrote were such standards as "Will You Love Me In December as You Do in May?" (written with Mayor James J. Walker of New York), "Mother Machree," "When Irish Eyes Are Smiling," "Let the Rest of the World Go By," and "A Little Bit of Heaven, Sure They Call It Ireland." (WRHS)

SPATS, TOPPERS, AND ASCOT TIES were the order of the day in 1901 when some members of the Four-in-Hand & Tandem Club gathered on the steps of the home of Charles A. Otis in Bratenahl. The dandies in the front row were Will White. Charles A. Otis, W. L. Rice, and James H. Hoyt; rear row, Belden Seymour, Dean Holden, A. F. (Burt) Holden, Dan R. Hanna, Sr., E. A. Merritt, Jacob B. Perkins, and Howard M. Hanna. (CPL)

DEMOCRACY ON WHEELS: The voting booths were mobile facilities in the early years of the twentieth century, and while they weren't very elegant, the driver, wearing a cutaway style wing-tip collar, and a stylish derby, does give the operation a touch of class worthy of Ward 32, Precinct C. (WRHS)

DOWNTOWN CLEVELAND was gayly decorated for the annual encampment of the Grand Army of the Republic, some thirty-five thousand strong, in September 1901, when news of the death of Pres. William McKinley broke. The eagle-topped decorative pylons lining the streets and the Public Square were hastily draped in black crepe and became symbols of mourning as the old soldiers of the Civil War joined Clevelanders in an expression of public grief. The photograph shows the Square on the day of McKinley's funeral. (Plain Dealer)

THE WEDDING OF THE CENTURY so far as Cleveland and much of the nation were concerned was the brilliant June 1903 marriage of Ruth Hanna, daughter of the famous Sen. Marcus A. Hanna, to Medill McCormick of Chicago. Among those who attended the nuptials in Saint Paul's Church, East Fortieth Street and Euclid Avenue, was Pres. Theodore Roosevelt. Shown in this wedding breakfast photograph, to the right of the bride, are Medill McCormick; Alice Roosevelt (later Mrs. Nicholas Longworth), daughter of the President; Mrs. Howard Hanna; and Miss Eleanor Patterson (later Countess Gizycka). Standing directly behind the bride is J. M. Patterson, later publisher of *Liberty Magazine* and the *New York Daily News*. To the left of the bride are Miss Lucia McCurdy (Mrs. Malcolm L. McBride), cousin and maid of honor to the bride; Col. Robert McCormick, publisher of the *Chicago Tribune*; and Robert Allerton of Chicago. Sitting second from the left is Bascom Little, with Miss Florence Cobb (the future Mrs. Bascom Little) to his right. Howard Hanna is standing farthest left. (Edmondson)

HAIL TO THE CHIEF! When Pres. Theodore Roosevelt was in Cleveland for the marriage of U. S. Sen. Marcus A. Hanna's daughter, Ruth, to Medill McCormick of Chicago in 1903, he was so impressed by the commanding appearance of Cleveland's police chief, Fred Kohler, that he said: "I believe you have the best chief of police in America in Kohler!" Chief Kohler, who later became mayor, posed with the President during that historic visit. (Baus)

AS MARK HANNA LAY DYING in January 1904, the famous cartoonist Homer Davenport drew this picture of America's death watch over the illustrious political leader from Cleveland. The shadowy figure to the right of Uncle Sam is Pres, William McKinley, Sen. Hanna's bosom friend and himself the victim of an assassin's bullets only a few years before. (News)

FUNERAL SERVICES for former U. S. Secretary of State John Hay drew a top representation of Washington officialdom— including Pres. Theodore Roosevelt—to Cleveland. The services were held in the old headquarters building of the Cleveland Chamber of Commerce on Public Square on July 5, 1905. The President and other dignitaries are shown leaving the building after the services. (Baus)

THE BIG POLITICAL ISSUE in Cleveland in 1906 centered on a battle for transit rights between Mayor Johnson's low-fare Forest City Railway and the consolidated opposition known as the Con-Con. When the Con-Con sought an injunction to prevent the Johnson line from reaching the Public Square, the mayor ordered workmen to lay temporary tracks over the pavement in an overnight blitz. The temporary poles to hold the overhead trolley lines were wedged in barrels propped between wagon wheels. The view is looking west on Superior Avenue, west of Public Square. (Plain Dealer)

IN MAY 1896, *The Plain Dealer* and the *Evening Post* took up headquarters in this building at the corner of Bond Street (East Sixth Street) and Superior Avenue. This is a 1906 photograph when *The Plain Dealer* enjoyed the largest morning circulation and Sunday circulation in the city and, as the sign on the side of the building modestly puts it, "No breakfast is complete without it." The chalk board hanging over the front entrance carries news bulletins of the day. (Plain Dealer)

MAYOR JOHNSON and some fellow dignitaries shown in the mayor's famous Winton automobile called the "Red Devil," sometime around 1906. (Baus)

GENERALLY CONCEDED is the fact that Tom L. Johnson was Cleveland's greatest mayor, and that Fred Kohler was Cleveland's greatest police chief. They are shown here together in a review of the Police Department on Superior Avenue in front of the old City Hall around 1905. (Plain Dealer)

NOT FOR NOTHING was Peter Witt known as the "stormy petrel" of Cleveland politics during the first three decades of the twentieth century. Witt, shown in characteristic fighting pose, became a lieutenant of the famous Tom L. Johnson and later made an unsuccessful bid for the mayor's seat himself. The area of public service in which he made his most lasting reputation was as traction commissioner of the city. (Plain Dealer)

MAYOR TOM L. JOHNSON was at the peak of his political power when he addressed an outdoor meeting about 1908. (Baus)

A LOT OF HORSEPOWER was needed to pull this handsome, twenty-one passenger coach parked in front of the old Hollenden Hotel sometime during the Tom L. Johnson administration. Mayor Johnson is in the center seat on top, farthest to the rear. The man wearing the derby on the back seat (to the extreme right) is Carl T. Robertson, a speechwriter for the mayor and later associate editor of *The Plain Dealer.* (Peter Carroll Photo)

[64]

PARADES provided great civic entertainment in the old days, and any reasonable excuse apparently brought out the bands and the marchers on the run. This civic parade on May 20, 1905, preceded the laying of the cornerstone of the new Federal Building. Its site is to the extreme left, behind the fence. The large building facing Superior Avenue in the center of the picture is the old Case Block, which for a long time contained the rented quarters of City Hall. (Baus)

SIGHTSEEING IN STYLE was made possible by this elegant horseless touring vehicle shown awaiting customers on Public Square around 1905. (Plain Dealer)

A STILL LIFE PHOTO apparently was enough to sell the 1905 Winton automobile made in Cleveland by Alexander Winton, famous automotive pioneer. (Wager)

"THE DUCHESS OF DIAMONDS" is what the newspaper writers at the turn of the century called Mrs. Cassie L. Chadwick. Claiming to be the illegitimate daughter of Andrew Carnegie, she swindled bankers and financiers in Cleveland, Pittsburgh, New York, and Boston of at least $2 million. She was convicted of fraud in 1905, and died in the Ohio State Penitentiary two and one-half years later. (Plain Dealer)

HELLO CENTRAL! This is the nerve center of the main telephone exchange of the Bell System in Cleveland in 1905. (Bell)

A POPULAR WATERING SPOT for Clevelanders with an appetite for hearty food and drink was Liederkranz Hall saloon at East Seventy-second Street and Kinsman Avenue. Under the Management of Ed Sohm from 1907 to 1910 and then his brother, George Sohm, until 1912, the Liederkranz, no cheesey establishment, did its best to keep its customers happy with free soup from nine in the morning to noon, a free lunch from noon through the afternoon, and free Hasenfeffer through the evening hours. Beer was five cents for a sixteen-ounce glass, while whiskey sold for five cents a shot, ten cents for a double shot. Anyone tiring of the food and drink could work it off at the Omaha Club Dance Hall upstairs. (Plain Dealer)

ABOUT TO TAKE A CANTER one fine day in 1907 were Cyrus S. Eaton, right, already famous as a utilities tycoon despite his youth, and his uncle, the Rev. Charles A. Eaton, then pastor of the church attended by John D. Rockefeller, the Euclid Avenue Baptist Church at East Eighteenth and Euclid. The Reverend Dr. Eaton later served a Baptist congregation in New York, and went on to become a United States congressman, representing a New Jersey district. After World War II, he was one of the authors of the United Nations Charter. (C&O)

A WIND-WHIPPED FIRE on the bitterly cold morning of February 2, 1908, destroyed the Plain Dealer Building, but publication was not interrupted because the other newspapers, *The Leader, The News,* and *The Press,* offered their stricken rival the use of their equipment. Publication continued in the News Building until temporary facilities could be established in the abandoned livery stable of Hotel Hollenden across Superior Avenue. (Plain Dealer)

ANOTHER TRAGEDY struck on the morning of March 4, 1908. A flash fire, which broke out shortly after classes had begun, destroyed Lakeview Elementary School on East 152nd Street in Collinwood and took a toll of 174 lives. Among those who died were 171 children, two teachers, and an unidentified man. The fire started in the basement under the front stairway. Many of the children panicked as they were marched down a rear stairway and encountered difficulty at the exit. Only one of the double doors was open. The other was fastened at the top with a spring. The bodies of the children were found stacked in front of the doorway. As the news spread, anxious parents gathered at the red brick schoolhouse, just seven years old. Twenty-one unidentified bodies were buried together in Lakeview Cemetery. (Plain Dealer)

ONLY FOUR MONTHS after the terrible school fire disaster in Collinwood had shocked the nation, another tragic fire occurred in Cleveland on July 3, 1908. Seven persons died and scores were injured when a fireworks counter in the S. S. Kresge five-and-ten-cent store at 2025 Ontario Street exploded. Cause of the explosion and fire was a child carrying a burning sparkler. The disaster led to nationwide legislation towards the banning of fireworks for private sale and the promotion of campaigns for a "safe and sane Fourth." (Plain Dealer)

A TORNADO ripped through Cleveland's East Side in late April 1909, and this was the aftermath scene in the wake of the twister somewhere in the vicinity of suburban Euclid. (WRHS)

THERE WASN'T MUCH yacht traffic around the old Cleveland Yacht Club at the foot of East Ninth Street on this day in 1909, and there was hardly a ripple on Lake Erie. (CPL)

B'NAI JESHURUN, a Hungarian synagogue, stood on the southeast corner of Willson Avenue (East Fifty-fifth) and Scovill Avenue, seen in 1909. (CPL)

AVIATION PIONEER Glenn Curtiss sped along the sands of Euclid Beach on August 31, 1910, in the beginning of an epochal flight all the way to Cedar Point, some sixty miles distant along Lake Erie, as a crowd estimated at 150,000 persons looked on. Curtis had hoped to break his previous speed record of fifty-two miles an hour in this flight, but "unfavorable winds" thwarted him. (WRHS)

PROGRESS brought with it, among other things, a dump *(above)* that sat on the downtown lakefront at the foot of Erie Street (East Ninth Street). One of the residents of the dump made the most of his situation in 1911 with his own flagpole, an official street sign, and a stern "No Admittance" notice *(right)*. Part of the lettering on the pennant reads "Class A." Class A dump? (CPL)

THE TANK WAGONS for hauling products of the Standard Oil Company to consumers were built in the company's wagon works in the Cleveland Flats. The two men posing in the center in this 1910 photo apparently were the big wheels. (Sohio)

WOMEN'S STYLES in 1911 are modeled here by members of the Women's Club of Trinity Episcopal Cathedral as they chat in front of the church after a meeting. (CPL)

GOLF was a rich man's game at the turn of the century, and the richest man on the links was John D. Rockefeller. With him about 1907 on this round were, at extreme left, the Rev. Charles A. Eaton, pastor of the Euclid Avenue Baptist Church and uncle of Cyrus S. Eaton, and, next to him, John D.'s favorite golfing partner and personal physician, Dr. H. F. Bigger. The identities of the other men are unknown. (Kraffert)

IN SUMMER, Mr. and Mrs. John D. Rockefeller almost always returned to their Forest Hill home in Cleveland. Photographer Andrew J. Kraffert, a personal favorite of the world's richest man, was on hand to snap this arrival at the East Cleveland train station, sometime around 1910. (Kraffert)

ROCKEFELLER GETS READY for a ride home in his horseless carriage after attending services at the Euclid Avenue Baptist Church about 1910. The long duster was standard wear for motorists. John D. also wore paper vests underneath his coat for extra warmth. (Kraffert)

FORE! John D. Rockefeller, perhaps the best-dressed golfer in the world on this particular day, gauges the direction of his drive during a not-so-private round in 1912 on his Forest Hill golf course. (Kraffert)

AN UNUSUAL PHOTOGRAPHIC STUDY of John D. Rockefeller as the multi-millionaire's car stopped in front of the Euclid Avenue Baptist Church, circa 1912. (Kraffert)

PRES. WILLIAM HOWARD TAFT *(above)* was the passenger at rear center, with mustache, in this touring car on a visit to Cleveland around 1912. Presidential security precautions were a lot looser in those days and the crowd has Taft hemmed in. The police officer standing on the running board at left was Police Chief Fred Kohler. Another shot of President Taft *(left)* during a 1912 visit to Cleveland shows him with a Major Butt as the officer on the left. Next to him, alongside the President, is Myron T. Herrick, who later distinguished himself as the United States ambassador to France. (Baus-Kraffert)

ONE INVENTION HELPS ANOTHER; Workmen of the Illuminating Company show off the company's first motorized overhead-lines truck in 1912. (CEIC)

HAIL TO THE CHAMP! Cleveland's first professional boxing champion, Johnny Kilbane, was one of the most outstanding in the history of the fight game. Kilbane, arm outstretched in greeting, is shown here with his manager, Jimmy Dunn (left), in a triumphant ride through the streets of Cleveland upon their return from California where Kilbane had beat Abe Attell for the featherweight title on February 22, 1912. The Cleveland fighter held the championship for more than eleven years, finally losing it to Eugene Crique of France on June 2, 1923. (Plain Dealer)

READY FOR BUSINESS in 1913, with spittoons lined up in military order, is Ross Armour's Saloon at West Twenty-fifth Street and Bridge Avenue. The distinction claimed by this establishment was that it was the first saloon in Cleveland to serve a free lunch featuring a whole fish and one slice of bread with each and every five-cent glass of beer. The bar was seventy feet long, and there were more than one hundred barrels and kegs stacked behind the bar to keep pace with the demands of the thirsty fish-eaters. (Helms)

THE VIOLENT SPRINGTIME WEATHER of 1913 had disastrous effects in a widespread area of the Midwest, and Cleveland was not spared. The flooding Cuyahoga caused the steamer *William H. Mack* to be torn from its moorings; out of control, it crashed into the West Third Street Bridge and put the span out of commission. One of the maritime hazards resulting from the excessive rain and flooding was that tons of lumber floated out of the riverside lumber yards and into the river and lake. (Plain Dealer)

[76]

THE BIG BLIZZARD of 1913, which began on November 9 and continued for three days, is one the oldtimers still talk about in Cleveland. Two feet of snow fell on the city on November 11, crippling transportation, causing roofs to cave in, and toppling service poles. Seventy-five percent of the electric power was knocked out and the city was buried and battered, as this aftermath photograph below shows. At the end of that storm in which more than twenty-two inches of snow fell, winds reaching as high as sixty miles an hour whipped the drifts into ten-foot peaks, bowled over pedestrians, stopped streetcars and private vehicles, and otherwise paralyzed the city for a full week *(facing page)*. (CEIC-WRHS)

THE COUNTY COURTHOUSE was brand new in 1913, and a lovely strip of Lakeview Park on the slope to the north of the beautiful building gave Clevelanders an ideal spot for lake watching. (Plain Dealer)

THE EAST SIDE and the West Side of Cleveland, separated by the Cuyahoga Valley, were joined by the Superior Viaduct from 1878 to 1916. This is how it looked shortly before it was replaced by the High Level Bridge, connecting Superior Avenue on the east with Detroit Avenue and West Twenty-fifth Street on the west. The old viaduct, while a masterful creation in its day, was a source of terrible annoyance because its center section, over the Cuyahoga River, would pivot open to allow large boats to pass through, and the delays in the traffic flow were maddening. (Baus)

THE INTERSECTION of East 105th and Euclid made history in 1914 when the first traffic signals were installed at the busy uptown corner. Notice the explanatory sign dangling from the overhead lines in the center of the street. (CAC)

AS FAMILIAR A LANDMARK in Cleveland as the Terminal Tower is the Detroit-Superior High Level Bridge, shown here in December 1915 at mid-construction stage. This high span replaced the Superior Viaduct as the major traffic link between east and west. A double-deck structure, it carried until recent times both motor traffic and pedestrians on its top level and streetcars on its underdeck. It is 3,112 feet in length, with 12 concrete arches and one 591-foot steel arch. It was the largest double-deck, reinforced concrete bridge in the world when it was opened in 1917. (Baus)

AN EXPLOSION on July 4, 1916, in the waterworks tunnel under Lake Erie leading to the Five-Mile Crib, killed the eleven trapped workmen who were extending the tunnel, and claimed the lives of ten other men who tried to save the workers. This was the scene in the harbor as the bodies of the victims were brought in *(below)*. The hero of the disaster was a black man named Garrett Morgan, who was credited with saving the lives of several men trapped in the tunnel. Morgan, an inventor, had devised a gas mask which enabled him and other rescuers to enter the waterworks crib in the lake and descend to the tunnel. Later, in 1922, Morgan invented the traffic signal light, patented that year. He is shown at left fingering one of several medals awarded him for his heroism in the crib explosion by the Cleveland Association of Colored Men and the International Association of Fire Chiefs. (Cleveland News-Baus)

THE AFFAIRS of the City of Cleveland were conducted for forty-one years from rented quarters in the big Case Block on Superior Avenue, shown here as it looked just before its demolition in 1916. The Public Library stands on the site. (Plain Dealer)

DURING A CLEVELAND RALLY in behalf of the Third Liberty Loan Drive of World War I, a guest speaker was the famous labor organizer Samuel Gompers, the short man in the center. The scowling man on his left under the derby is Cleveland's mayor (later Ohio governor), Harry L. Davis. (Baus)

AN EXPOSITION of World War I trophies captured from the Germans was a popular attraction downtown, probably to spur Liberty Bond sales. Some of the exhibits, like this German cannon *(below),* appealed immensely to cutups in the crowd like the ones shown here. There really wasn't much left of the captured German airplane *(left),* but even the debris was thrilling. (WRHS)

THE UNIFORM worn by Uncle Sam's doughboys in World War I apparently was called on to do double duty at war's end, as the costume of this Cleveland mailman would suggest. (Plain Dealer)

THE NEW PLAIN DEALER BUILDING, constructed on the site of the old one on the block from Superior Avenue to Rockwell Avenue, along Bond Street (East Sixth), was built in three stages. The Rockwell section was built first to accommodate the presses and technical equipment. The Superior addition was not completed until November 1911. In 1921, with the city booming, work was begun to double the size of the newspaper building by an addition along Superior Avenue that would reach all the way back to Rockwell. The newspaper occupied this building until 1956. It then became a wing of the Cleveland Public Library. (Plain Dealer)

EDGEWATER PARK on the West Side looked like this early in the century before land fill created a sports recreational area to the north, pushing back the shoreline. The roadway on the left is Bulkley Boulevard, the forerunner of the West Memorial Shoreway. The ornate Edgewater Bath House may be seen in the distance at center. (CPL)

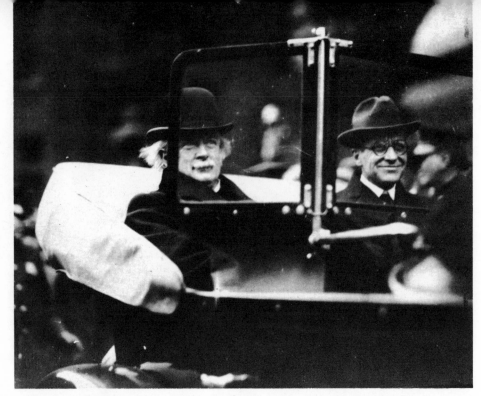

ENGLAND'S PRIME MINISTER, David Lloyd George, was one of the post-World War I visitors to Cleveland. His riding companion is the former mayor and ex-secretary of war, Newton D. Baker. (Plain Dealer)

DANCE HALLS WERE BUSY PLACES in the Turbulent Twenties, and in 1920 this dance pavilion in Edgewater Park was one of the "in" places for the flappers and the sheiks of that day. (Plain Dealer)

THE FIRST ROAD in the Rocky River Reservation of the Cleveland Metropolitan Park System: The river once ran where the dirt road was built. (CAC)

BANK ROBBING was hard, risky work at the time this picture was taken in suburban Bedford on October 21, 1920. The Cleveland Trust Company branch bank had just been the target of a gang of six gunmen headed by an infamous outlaw of the time, George (Jiggs) Losteiner. As the holdup was in progress, however, a bank clerk set off the burglar alarm, bringing a small army of indignant citizens to the scene. The result was a pitched, if one-sided, battle between the would-be bank robbers and the militant townspeople. One of the criminals died and three were wounded in the melee, promptly dubbed "The Battle of Bedford." (Plain Dealer)

PIONEER PUZZLE: Legend has it that when the founding party from Connecticut arrived at the place where the Cuyahoga River flows into Lake Erie, the predetermined site of their settlement, they found a log cabin at the mouth of the river on its west bank. It was said to be a trading post owned by the Astor family. This ancient, ill-used building once stood in the Cleveland Flats and was said to be the old log structure in clapboard dress. Its sentimental value was not high in the city that grew up around it and, historical or not, it was torn down as an eyesore in 1922. (Plain Dealer)

HERO'S END: Ray Chapman was one of the stars of the Cleveland Indians team that won the American League pennant in 1920, but he wasn't around to enjoy the ultimate triumph. Chapman, a brilliant shortstop, was killed by a pitch thrown by New York Yankee pitcher Carl Mays on August 16 during a game in the Polo Grounds in New York. He was buried from Saint John's Cathedral as thousands of saddened Clevelanders filled the church and jammed East Ninth Street and Superior Avenue during the funeral services. (Plain Dealer)

ONE OF THE FANCIEST bathhouses in the nation stood at the water's edge at Edgewater Beach in its most elegant days. The year was 1922, and if Lake Erie was polluted, nobody had noticed it. Picnic benches accommodated non-bathers on the rooftop pavilion of the remarkable recreational structure, torn down shortly after World War II. (News)

A WARTIME TEAM REUNITED: Gen. John J. Pershing, visiting Cleveland on February 14, 1922, was greeted by the former mayor of the city, to his left, Newton D. Baker—who also had served as secretary of war in the cabinet of Pres. Woodrow Wilson during World War I. (Plain Dealer)

CENTRAL POLICE STATION is shown here as it looked when it stood on Champlain Street, to the southwest of Public Square. Both the headquarters building and the street itself were eliminated in 1922 by the Terminal Tower complex that was built by the Van Sweringen brothers. (Plain Dealer)

[87]

THE END WAS IN SIGHT for a street scene like this one taken on November 24, 1922. It shows the southwest corner of Public Square, and the buildings were demolished shortly thereafter to make way for the new Higbee Company store and the Terminal Tower. (News)

FORMALITY was the order of the day in radio in 1924 for the WHK studio orchestra. Mrs. Max Schmidt is at the organ, left. Also in the group are Hans Kobel and Max Schmidt. The names of the other two men are not known. (WHK)

POLITICAL EXCITEMENT stirred Cleveland in early summer 1924 when the Republican Party held its convention in the city's brand-new Public Auditorium. Some ten thousand delegates and visitors gathered on June 10 in the big hall *(above).* Large crowds filled the city streets, and amid all the usual hoopla surrounding political conventions were, naturally, live elephants, seen here in front of the old Armory on East Sixth Street. Special pylon decorations had been put up for the occasion, as on crowd-filled East Sixth Street *(below),* looking north toward City Hall. (Plain Dealer)

CALVIN COOLIDGE was the nominee of the 1924 Republican Convention, and Cartoonist Hal Donahey of *The Cleveland Plain Dealer* reacted to the victory of the former governor of Massachusetts with this cartoon. (Plain Dealer)

[90]   THIS AERIAL VIEW shows Euclid Beach Amusement Park as it looked in 1924. It was out in the country then, and its famous beach had not yet been badly damaged by erosion, but the dark line at water's edge suggests that pollution was not unknown even at that early date.

THE FRONT YARD of the Cleveland Museum of Art was not so artistic in 1924, before the beautiful lagoon and promenade were built. (Plain Dealer)

THE PRESIDENT OF THE CITY Council under the city-manager form of government in 1924 was the city's ceremonial mayor, and Clayton Townes, who held that post, did his duty by posing with a famous young visitor, Jackie Coogan. (Plain Dealer)

THIS LAKEFRONT VIEW in the 1920s, northward from Superior Avenue and East Ninth Street, shows in the foreground the old Saint John's Cathedral, the mother church of the Cleveland Catholic diocese, as it looked before the extensive rebuilding program in the post-World War II period. Especially prominent in the appearance of the old cathedral, dedicated in 1852, was its high steeple, removed in the later renovation. The grade school, lower right, was torn down. The building occupied by *The Cleveland Press* was diagonally across East Ninth Street, at the corner of Rockwell Avenue. (Plain Dealer)

Cleveland from 1925 to 1950

ONE OBSERVER who was more impressed than most by the incredible growth of the Forest City, it seems, was Prof. J. Paul Goode of the University of Chicago. A nationally respected geographer, Dr. Goode predicted in 1925 that Cleveland eventually would take its place as one of the three great urban centers of the entire world.

It did look, at the time, as if the city were seriously aiming at some such high estate in the world scheme of things. There was much excitement in Cleveland in 1925. The new public library, third largest in the United States, opened that year, and bulldozers were clearing 1,000 acres of farmland west of the city, beginning construction of the biggest municipal airfield in the world.

The new Terminal Tower complex, transforming Public Square and upper Euclid Avenue from East Twelfth to East Eighteenth streets, was becoming the glittering center of entertainment called Playhouse Square, as some of the most beautiful movie houses in the country sprang into being (including the Palace, State, Allen, Stillman, and Lake theaters). The aristocratic Hanna Theater, a home of stage productions, stood regally off to one side on East Fourteenth.

Cleveland was big, young, brawny, and a winner all the way in that day of heady success and well-being. But Cleveland, like every other American city, was in for the toughest fight of its life. The stock market crash of 1929 and the depression of the 1930s dropped Cleveland to one knee, and there were times in the years that followed when even its most enthusiastic boosters were ready to concede the ten-count.

Even so, the 1930s were surprisingly eventful years. The convention of the Republican Party in 1936, the annual National Air Races, the Eucharistic Congress held in Cleveland Municipal Stadium in September 1935, and the Great Lakes Exposition, staged on lake-fill land along two miles of the Cleveland lakefront in 1936-37, all distracted Clevelanders from the economic miseries of the time, and focused national attention on the city.

But the long, enervating depression had sapped the city's strength and optimism by the time 1940 rolled around. The city's morale sagged, but not all the signs were negative. There was still growth, not the prairie-wildfire kind of expansion that had become commonplace during the previous eighty years, but impressive growth, nevertheless.

By 1940, Cleveland occupied some thirty-five miles of Lake Erie shoreline, and Cuyahoga County had a population of 1,217,250, making it ninth largest county in the United States. But Clevelanders were shocked by the census tabulation that year. It recorded the first population loss in the city's history; a backward slip to 878,336 that dropped Cleveland to sixth place.

It dropped another notch in 1950 to seventh, even though there was a slight rally that pushed the population count to 914,808. In all fairness, the official census didn't reflect the true growth of the metropolitan area. Greater Cleveland, by 1950, sprawled out over a three-county area that included Lake, Lorain, and Cuyahoga counties, and contained more than sixty-six suburbs, depending on where one chose to draw the line. Within this area lived more than 2,000,000 persons.

Moses would have been amazed.

SOCIETY FOLLOWED a hard line on drinking and gambling alike during the Prohibition days, and policemen carried a big stick, usually a sledge hammer. Police Chief Jacob Graul posed here for one of the favorite newspaper pictures of the era, as he pounded some seized slot machines into rubble. (News)

NO EARLY SPACE MACHINE off the drawing board of a mad genius inventor this, but a truck loaded with equipment seized in a police raid on a bootleg whiskey distillery in February 1929. (News)

[94]

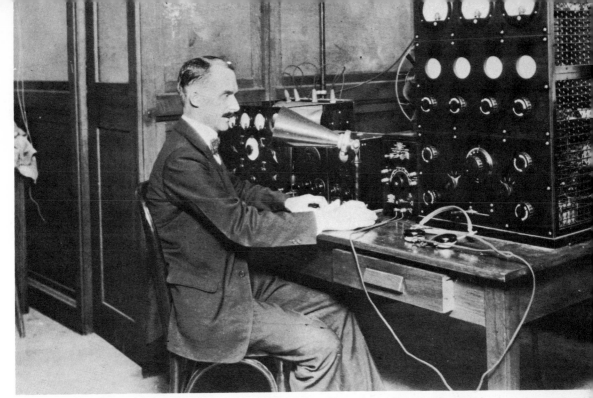

A 1924 RADIO BROADCASTER was famous Cleveland economist and business analyst, Col. Leonard P. Ayres, as he passed along his expert opinion to listeners from the studios of WHK. Note the funnel-type microphone, scientifically designed to catch every word. Station WHK was the first commercial radio station in Ohio, having begun regular broadcasts on July 26, 1921. (WHK)

A PRE-TELEVISION SPORTS ATTRACTION was the scoreboard mounted on the front of the Illuminating Company building to provide play-by-play reports on the 1927 World Series. Thousands of Clevelanders gathered on the Public Square lawn every afternoon to follow the action. (CEIC)

THE GLENN L. MARTIN COMPANY, manufacturer of heavy bomber planes, made Cleveland an important center of aviation production in the 1920s. This biplane with the silver wings, *The City of Cleveland*, was built by Martin to carry Cleveland's message as an air center to the International Aviation Peace Jubilee at Santa Anna, California in June 1927. Clifford Gildersleeve, secretary of the aviation committee of the Cleveland Chamber of Commerce, is shown (left) with the pilot, Kenneth R. Cole.

THE MOST THRILLING STREETCAR RIDE in town—one of the best in the country until streetcars were abandoned in 1954—took passengers of the Cleveland Railway Company and, later, the Cleveland Transit System, down this subway on West Superior Avenue *(above)* and over the Cuyahoga River on an underdeck *(below)* of the huge Detroit-Superior High Level Bridge. (News)

A TRAFFIC TOWER with a policeman inside and traffic lights mounted in the top and sides was a 1925 answer to the problem of automobile and pedestrian traffic at the intersection of East Ninth Street and Euclid Avenue, described at the time as one of the busiest intersections in the world. It was not a satisfactory answer, however, and the tower was removed in 1931 as a traffic hazard itself. (CAC)

WATCH THE BIRDIE is what photographer Andrew J. Kraffert of the *Plain Dealer* presumably is telling the lion in the Brookside Zoo cage as he takes his picture one fine day in 1925. (Plain Dealer)

TORN DOWN in 1926 to make way for the new Ohio Bell Telephone Company Building were these famous Cleveland landmarks, the Empire Burlesque Theater, left, and the old Huron Road Hospital on the right. (Bell)

THE NEW TERMINAL TOWER with its fifty-two stories, was nearing completion in 1927. The photograph was made from the roof of the equally new Ohio Bell Telephone Company Building on Huron Road. (CPL)

THE COMPLETED UNION TERMINAL project of the Van Sweringen brothers, as seen here in part, was approximately eleven years in the making. The 35-acre land site began in 1919 and took several years. Actual construction began in 1923 and was not completed until 1930. The estimated cost was $200 million. The Terminal Tower, 708 feet high, stood for many years as the tallest skyscraper in the United States outside of New York City and the eighth tallest building in the world. (Brumbach)

IT WAS A BUSY DAY in September 1928 when the photographer caught this street scene near the West Side Market on West Twenty-fifth Street. (Plain Dealer)

A DISASTER occurred at the Cleveland Clinic *(below)* on May 15, 1929. Burning X-ray films in a basement storage room inside the building at East Ninety-third Street and Euclid Avenue emitted a lethal combination of gases that killed a total of 124 persons, including nine doctors. Investigators later surmised that a bare light bulb on an extension cord had been left on a shelf too close to the X-ray film. One of the fire department investigators is shown *(left)* as he sifted through the ashes of the films. (Plain Dealer)

VICTIMS of the Cleveland Clinic fire were attended on the lawn of the famous institution during the 1929 disaster. (Seid)

FRANTIC FRIENDS and relatives gathered at the old County Morgue on Lakeside Avenue, near East Ninth Street, in the wake of the Cleveland Clinic disaster on May 16, 1929. The morgue was torn down when the site was cleared to make way for the 33-story Federal Building of the Erieview Urban Renewal project in the 1960s. (News)

MANY GENERATIONS of Clevelanders found their fun and recreation at Luna Park, an amusement park off Woodland Avenue and East Ninty-third Street. This is a 1929 view. The park included a sports stadium where John Carroll University played its home football games. The park was demolished in the 1930s. (News)

CHARLES A. LINDBERGH was a visitor to Cleveland in August 1927, when public excitement was still at a peak over his successful flight across the Atlantic in May of that year. Among those in the welcoming committee were (extreme left) Edwin Barry, city safety director, and (right) John D. Marshall, president of City Council and ceremonial mayor. (Seid)

THREE FAMOUS PILOTS came together at Municipal Airport in 1929. They were Navy flier Lt. Al Williams, Charles A. Lindbergh, and Lt. James (Jimmy) Doolittle.

MARINE STUNT FLIERS were executing their dare-devil maneuvers over Cleveland Airport during the National Air Races of 1928 when Herman Seid took this photograph from the end plane. He got sick, but he didn't let that interfere with his picture-taking. (Seid)

AVIATION was still struggling to get out of its swaddling clothes in 1929, but Clevelanders enjoyed daily seaplane service to Detroit from the old yacht basin near the East Ninth Street docks. (Meli)

AVIATION PIONEERS Glenn L. Martin and Charles A. Lindbergh meet at the 1929 National Air Races. (Plain Dealer)

IN THIS PILOT GROUPING on the field of Cleveland Airport during the 1929 National Air Races were (left to right) Maj. Thomas J. Herbert of the Army Air Corps reserve, Lt. James (Jimmy) Doolittle, and Lt. C. M. Cummings. Major Herbert later became governor of Ohio. Lieutenant Doolittle became a general and bombed the Japanese. (News)

THE LARGEST CROWD ever to attend an air show in the United States at the time, more than 100,000 persons, is shown in this aerial view of the municipal airport in Cleveland on August 28, 1929. (Wilk)

ONE OF THE THRILLS overhead in the 1929 National Air Races held in Cleveland was the transfer of a passenger from an airship, the U.S.S. *Los Angeles,* to an airplane. Lieutenant Bolster performed the feat, going from the dirigible into the tiny Vought biplane hooked on to the underside of the *Los Angeles.*

JUST A SPECTATOR at the 1929 National Air Races at Municipal Airport was Dr. Hugo Eckener, the famous German dirigible expert, who is standing behind the WTAM microphone looking upward. To his left, concentrating on the air action, is City Manager William R. Hopkins, who later was honored when the airport's name was changed to Cleveland Hopkins International Airport.

THE FOOT OF East Ninth Street on the lakefront was a busy place when the old C & B and D & C lines were alive and operating boats between Cleveland and other major cities on the Great Lakes. As this June 8, 1929, photograph shows, streetcars were used to take passengers directly to the pier terminal building. (News)

PASSENGER TRAVEL via lake steamships was popular until World War II. The *City of Cleveland III*, one of the most popular boats on the lakes, was tied up near East Ninth Street on this clear day in October 1931. (News)

NEARING THE END: Two of the famous passenger boats that served Cleveland and other cities on the Great Lakes in the early decades of the century are shown at dock in the 1930s. In the left forefront is the popular *Seeandbee* of the Cleveland and Buffalo (C & B) Line. To the right rear is the *City of Erie,* also of the C & B Line. (Plain Dealer)

A NIGHTTIME SCENE in the glamorous Playhouse Square sometime during the 1930s: A clue to which year is the marquee of the Allen Theater advertising a Clara Bow movie, *Saturday Night Kid.* (Seid)

THE DEDICATION BANQUET of the new, $160-million Cleveland Union Terminal on June 28, 1930, was held in the central concourse of the terminal itself. Among the 2,500 guests from all over the United States were the presidents of virtually all the nation's railroads. (Wilk)

THE AIR WAS CLEAN AND CLEAR on this lovely summer afternoon in the early 1930s when Herman Seid stopped on the bluff just above Perkins Beach on the West Side and aimed his camera at the downtown Cleveland skyline in the distance. (Seid)

PALM TREES from light poles was the neat conversion effected on Public Square in 1931. The reason behind the tropical look has been lost. Cleveland College in the old Chamber of Commerce Building to the rear is gone now; it once stood on the north side of the Square, but it was cleared away to make room for a parking lot. (News)

RABID BASEBALL FANS followed the Cleveland Indians through radio play-by-play re-creations, broadcast at one time or another by stations WHK and WCLE. The star performers who made it sound as if they were watching the game from the press box were Pinky Hunter (left) and Jack Graney (center). The engineer (right) is unidentified. (Marcell)

A SPORTS-ANNOUNCING PIONEER in radio was Tom (Red) Manning of Cleveland, who teamed with the famous Graham McNamee in the play-by-play descriptions of many World Series games in the late 1920s and early 1930s. His career in Cleveland radio covered some forty years. (WTAM)

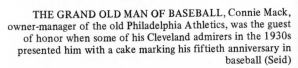

GENE & GLENN, a singing-comedy team, reached peak national popularity over the NBC Radio Network in the early 1930s, but Cleveland was their home base, and WTAM was their originating station. They are shown sifting through the fantastic mail that poured into the station from their fans. Glenn Rowell is on the left. With him is Gene Carroll. (News)

[109]

THE GRAND OLD MAN OF BASEBALL, Connie Mack, owner-manager of the old Philadelphia Athletics, was the guest of honor when some of his Cleveland admirers in the 1930s presented him with a cake marking his fiftieth anniversary in baseball (Seid)

FINALE FOR A FAMOUS FIREMAN: Fire Chief George A. Wallace (center, in white) is shown still stalwart and erect at his last fire, a store on Woodland Avenue, on February 19, 1931. He had joined the Cleveland Fire Department on June 1, 1869, and had become chief in 1901—a fantastic career span of sixty-two years! (Kraffert)

AN OUTSTANDING piece of sculpture by Clevelander Max Kalish, a statue of Abraham Lincoln, was placed facing the Mall in front of the Board of Education Building, and dedicated on Lincoln's birthday, February 12, 1932. (City)

FOR MORE THAN A DECADE after the huge Municipal Stadium was built, the Cleveland Indians
continued to play most of their games in their home park, Dunn Field, later renamed League Park.
The field at East Sixty-sixth and Lexington Avenue was old but a popular place with the fans because
of its intimate dimensions. The photograph shows it off to advantage as it looked on opening day,
April 1935, when a crowd of 21,500 filled the stands. (CPL)

STAR PITCHER Wesley Ferrell of the
Cleveland Indians is shown in the early
1930s flanked by some of Cleveland's
leading sports journalists and camera-
men. They are (left to right) Dan Taylor
of *The Cleveland News* and, later, *The
Cleveland Press*: Gordon Cobbledick, late
sports editor of *The Plain Dealer*: Ferrell;
Walter McNichols, secretary of the Cleveland Baseball Company; Perry Cragg, photographer for *The Cleveland News*: and
Charles Wilk, photographer for Wide
World Photos, Cleveland Bureau. (C&O)

[111]

ONE OF THE MOST SPECTACULAR FIRES in recent Cleveland history was this blaze in June 1932 that all but destroyed the Ellington Apartments at East Ninth Street and Superior Avenue downtown, killing ten persons and leaving thirteen missing. A series of explosions preceded the million-dollar nighttime fire. (Wilk)

MUNICIPAL AIRPORT was a busy place in 1934 after Pres. Franklin D. Roosevelt ordered the Army to fly the mail instead of the civilian carrier lines. These planes of the Army's air corps were clustered on the Cleveland airfield as preparations were rushed to assume the new assignment. In the foreground is a small pursuit plane with a mail capacity of only 100 pounds. To the right is one of the big bombing planes of the day, the last of the biplanes, with a bomb bay big enough to hold 4,000 pounds of mail. In the background is one of the first of a new breed of airplanes, the Martin Bomber.

ANOTHER VICTORY for the legendary Roscoe C. Turner occurred in the Thompson Trophy competition at the 1934 National Air Races. Presenting the coveted trophy to Colonel Turner at the end of the 100-mile race which he won at an average speed of 248 miles an hour is Frederick C. Crawford, president of Thompson Products Company. (Wilk)

THE UGLY, DESPERATE MOOD of the Depression is reflected in this street demonstration in Cleveland during the mid-1930s. Notice the sign over on the left, "Join the Communist Party." (City)

[114]

AN OUTSTANDING RELIGIOUS EXPRESSION in the United States during the twentieth century was the National Eucharistic Congress held in Cleveland in late September 1935. Some 22,000 people marched to Cleveland Stadium's playing field and formed a living monstrance, the receptacle in which the consecrated Host (body of Christ) is exposed for adoration, while an estimated one-hundred and fifty thousand Roman Catholic spectators looked on. The altar is in the center of the monstrance. (Plain Dealer)

A BATTERY OF MICROPHONES confronted Patrick Cardinal Hayes *(above)* of New York upon his arrival in Cleveland on September 24, 1935, for the National Eucharistic Congress. To the cardinal's right, wearing tall silk toppers, were Gov. Martin L. Davey of Ohio and Msgr. Joseph F. Smith of Saint John's Cathedral. To the left of the cardinal were Bishop Joseph Schrembs of Cleveland, Mayor Harry L. Davis, and Police Chief George J. Matowitz. Gov. Alfred E. Smith *(right)* of New York, 1928 Democratic Presidential candidate, knelt on the grass and said the rosary during the spectacular nighttime mass in the mammoth sports arena. Notice Smith's famous brown derby on the grass in front of his knees. Among the distinguished visitors *(below)* on the platform of Public Hall during one of the sessions of the nationwide meeting were (left to right) Jessica Dragonette, famous radio singer; Dr. R. P. Sullivan of New York; Governor Smith; and Governor Davey of Ohio.
(Plain Dealer-Wilk)

RADIO COMEDIAN JACK BENNY (with cat-cher's mask), not quite thirty-nine, and even younger than that, Joe Louis, heavyweight boxing champion, formed a crowd-pleasing battery in Cleveland Stadium on April 14, 1936, as the Indians and the Detroit Tigers met in the season opener, (Wilk)

SOME OF THE JEWELS in the famous University Circle area of Cleveland's East Side: In the center is the Cleveland Museum of Art, with its reflecting lagoon and fine arts garden, as it looked in 1936. The new Severance Hall, home of the Cleveland Orchestra, is on the right. Epworth Methodist Church is to the left of the lagoon. (Butler)

MORE THAN 10,000 Republicans again crowded into Cleveland on June 12, 1936, to nominate a candidate to oppose FDR. These "Uncle Sams" from Buffalo, New York, held up traffic on Euclid Avenue *(above)* while demonstrating their preference for Gov. Alfred Landon of Kansas. The happiest Republican in Cleveland was Alf Landon himself *(right)*, who arrived by train after he had been notified of his nomination as the GOP's standard-bearer. Alas, the happiness did not last—FDR won anyway. (Plain Dealer-Seid)

THE DEPRESSION YEARS were a time of labor unrest and widespread union organization in industrial plants. Cleveland saw its share of violence. One man was killed and sixty were injured in a clash at the Corrigan-McKinney plant of the Republic Steel Corporation between strikers and non-union workers in mid-summer of 1937. (Wilk)

THE BEST HEAVYWEIGHT FIGHTER to represent Cleveland during the golden years of boxing was Johnny Risko, who beat some of the best fighters of the 1920s and the 1930s, including Jack Sharkey, Paul Berlenbach, and George Godfrey. He was nearing the end of the fistic trail when this picture was taken in November 1937 following his victory over Bob Olin. Standing at his side in the moment of victory is his manager, Danny Dunn. (News)

INFORMALITY was the word of the day in radio in 1937 as Sid Andorn, veteran Cleveland newspaperman and radio performer, interviewed Sonja Henie. (Plain Dealer)

THE BRIGHT SPOT OF THE DEPRESSION in Cleveland was the colorful Great Lakes Exposition that for two years, 1936-37, transformed the downtown lakefront into funland. A large amount of land on which not only the exposition but also Municipal Stadium, at right, was built was freshly created by filling the beach and pushing it further into Lake Erie. This view *(above)* from the lake looks directly south to the end of the Mall. In the forefront is Billy Rose's Aquacade. In right foreground is the Horticultural Building. To left center, behind the boat, are the Hall of Progress and the Automotive Building. The aerial view *(below)* is looking east along the lakefront. (Wilk-WRHS)

THE AVENUE OF THE PRESIDENTS of the Great Lakes Exposition can be seen in this view looking north *(above)*. The Aquacade, one of the exposition's most popular attractions, had as its principals *(left)*, Billy Rose, Eleanor Holm, and Johnny Weissmueller, from left to right. The scene below shows the bandstand and concert area on the Mall, with the Public Auditorium and City Hall to the right. (WRHS)

PROHIBITION was still an unpleasant memory in the minds of the patrons of this workingman's saloon at East Seventy-ninth and Bessemer Avenue in 1937. Those prices posted on the backbar are enough to drive anyone to drink—14 cents for a shot of whiskey, 10 cents for a bottle of beer! (News)

CLEVELAND was the national center of amateur baseball during the 1920s and the 1930s, and Brookside Park's natural amphitheater was the place where most important games were played. An estimated 85,000 were on hand for this Class A game between the Poschke Barbecues and the Lyon Tailors in 1938. A world-record crowd of more than 100,000 jammed Brookside's hills to watch a game of amateur baseball between the White Autos and the Omaha, Nebraska, Luxus team on October 10, 1915. (Plain Dealer)

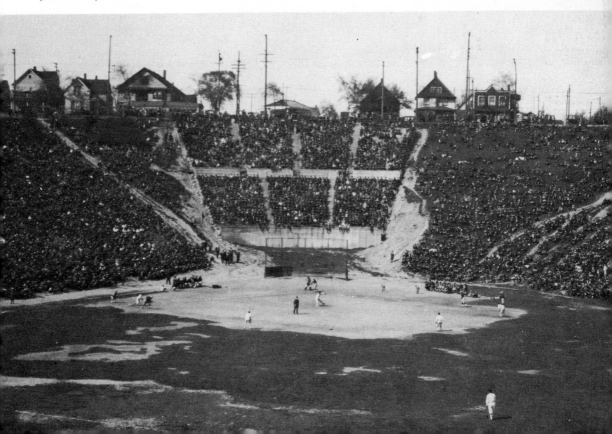

JESSE OWENS, TRACK IMMORTAL, was outstanding enough to draw national attention even as a high school runner at East Technical High School in the early 1930s. He established himself as a superstar in the world of track as a member of the Ohio State University team, reaching the collegiate pinnacle at the Western Conference Outdoor Track and Field Meet at Ann Arbor, Michigan, on May 25, 1935, in which he broke three world records and tied a fourth in a period of 45 minutes. The events were the 100-yard dash, broad jump, 220-yard dash, and the 220-yard low hurdles. But his biggest triumph was to be at the 1936 Olympics in Berlin, where, to the dismay of Adolf Hitler, Owens won three gold medals in record-breaking individual performances and helped the American 400-meter relay team win a fourth gold medal, again in record time. An Associated Press poll of the nation's sportswriters and sportscasters at mid-century named Owens the "greatest track athlete since 1900."

He is shown here *(left, above)* as he looked when he was a member of the East Tech track team; as an Ohio State star *(above)*; wearing an Olympic laurel wreath and showing the three gold medals he won in the Berlin Olympiad *(left, below)*; with his wife Ruth, being greeted as the returning hero in Cleveland in August 1936 *(facing page, top)*; and showing his speed, even weighed down by a baseball uniform *(facing page, bottom)*. He raced George Case, fleet Cleveland outfielder, in the 100-yard dash in Cleveland Stadium, and won in the remarkable time of 9.9 seconds. Case was timed at 10 seconds. (News)

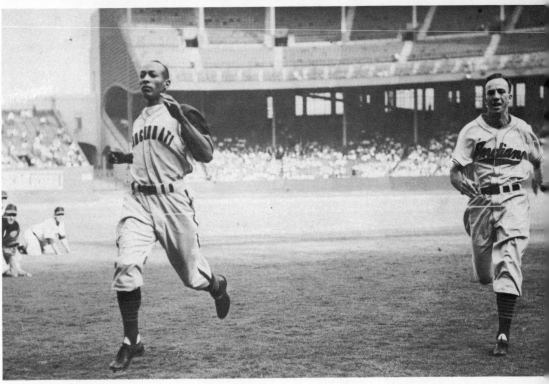

BOB HOPE was out of uniform when he kicked off the 1939 season of the Cleveland Rams, but everybody agreed that it was a funny kick. (Seid)

THE END OF THE ROCKY ROAD: The wrecking crews already were at work on the demolition of this former home of John D. Rockefeller on Euclid Avenue and East Fortieth Street when the picture was taken in 1938. Rockefeller bought the property in 1868 for $40,000, and four of his five children, Alta, Edith, John D., Jr., and Alice, were born in the house. (Plain Dealer)

A RELIEF CRISIS confronted city officials on this day in early May 1938, because Cleveland had exhausted its relief funds and the headlines said, "75,000 Clevelanders on Relief Face Starvation!" While Mayor E. Burton, later a justice of the U. S. Supreme Court, awaited help from the Ohio Legislature, some food from the federal surplus commodities agency was distributed to the destitute and hungry. Each person in this long line received a bag of oranges and apples and a pound of rice. (Wilk)

FUN ON LAKE ERIE, just off Cleveland harbor, as some ice boat enthusiasts skim along the frozen lake in the smoky 1930s (Seid)

JACK PAAR, wearing a stylish mustache in 1939, was an announcer on the staff of Station WGAR. (Condon)

LENDING AN EXOTIC NOTE to the Cleveland skyline to the south, not far from the busy downtown area, is this old Russian Orthodox church, Saint Theodosius, at 2547 St. Tichon Street. The photograph was taken in 1940. (CPL)

HOW! The arrival of Moses Cleaveland and his party was reenacted on the banks of the Cuyahoga River on Founders Day, July 22, 1941, with W. G. Oswald in the role of General Cleaveland and Chief Ghema Niagara portraying the friendly Indian Emissary. (News)

WITHIN DAYS after Pearl Harbor, Cleveland's patriotic young men hurried to volunteer for military service. The scene below is typical of the time, and was snapped in the Cleveland recruiting office of the U. S. Marine Corps. As the city rallied to the industrial challenge of World War II, its housewives became warworkers. Shown here *(left)* learning to be aircraft builders at the Cleveland Trade Aircraft School are Mrs. Estelle Tripolsky on the left and Mrs. Adeline Sietman as they rivet a sub-assembly. (News-Plain Dealer)

THE HEADLINES OF WORLD WAR II
lost their place on the front pages when a
large tank for the storage of liquefied
gas exploded on Cleveland's East Side on
October 20, 1944. A total of 131 persons lost their lives in the explosion and
the fires that leveled the neighborhoods
in the vicinity of the East Ohio Gas Company tank. The overall scene *(above)* of
the disaster shows the extent of damage
caused in the surrounding residential
neighborhood. Smoke is still pouring
from the exploded tank. Experts considered it something of a miracle that the
other storage tanks shown did not ex-
plode also. Rescuers *(right)* assist an injured man from the wreckage of his house
in which he was trapped after the explosion. (CPL)

THE CLEVELAND SKYLINE of 1945, as seen from the west side of the Cuyahoga Valley on a late summer day when the clouds were at their best. (Rebman)

V-E DAY, the surrender of Germany and the beginning of the end of World War II, was signaled by this headline hurriedly draped over a great billboard war map maintained on Public Square by the *Cleveland News.* (Cragg)

CLEVELAND'S BIG CELEBRATION was V-J Day. Thousands of jubilant people jammed into the downtown area when the big news came through in mid-August 1945, and the celebration lasted far into the night. Not even a rainfall could dampen the spirits of those who ranged the streets, singing and dancing. Among the most cheerful, naturally, were members of the armed forces, like the sailors and Waves *(above),* who formed a parade of their own. At the corner of East Ninth and Euclid Avenue, a barefoot soldier *(right)* hoisted a toast while his comrades smiled their approval. The formal parade *(below)* to celebrate the war's end was held in September, and one of the cars in it carried this distinguished complement of passengers: (left to right) Adm. Ernest J. King, commander of the Navy; Ohio Gov. Frank J. Lausche; U. S. Sen. Harold H. Burton; and Mayor Thomas A. Burke. (News)

THREE BASEBALL IMMORTALS, all identified with the Cleveland Indians, come together in Cleveland Municipal Stadium on the night of August 24, 1945, as pitcher Bob Feller's return to baseball is celebrated at the end of World War II. Helping to welcome back the young fireballer are Tris Speaker (center), one of the great center fielders of all time and former manager of the Indians, and Denton True (Cy) Young, the greatest baseball pitcher of all time. (Wilk)

THE BEGINNING OF THE BROWNS: Coach Paul Brown, fresh from wartime service as mentor of the Great Lakes Naval Training Station football team, arrived in Cleveland in 1946 to take up his new duties as the coach of a professional team that did not yet exist—the Cleveland Browns of the All-America Conference. Greeting Brown with a handshake is Arthur B. (Mickey) McBride, Cleveland taxicab magnate and owner of the Browns. Behind him is the coaching staff (left to right): Red Conkright, Fritz Heisler, John Brickels, and Bob Voigts. (News)

THE FIRST CHAMPIONSHIP of many to come was recorded in this All-America Conference game of 1946 in which the Cleveland Browns beat the New York Yankees, 14 to 9. Among the standout players for the Browns in the game was the man chosen by Coach Brown to break the color line in professional football, fullback Marion Motley, shown here as he ripped off a nine-yard gain. (News)

THE WEST SIDE MARKET, said to be the largest indoor market in the world and certainly the only one with an impressive campanile, also has a busy fringe element. These outdoor hucksters' stands are shown along the south side of the market building on Lorain Avenue, looking towards West Twenty-fifth Street in 1946. (Cragg)

A WEEKEND SHOPPING SCENE inside the vast West Side Market. The date was July 5, 1946, but it could have been any day before or since. (News)

AMONG THE MOST SPECTACULAR PLANES to compete in the last years of the National Air Races in Cleveland was the P-38 of World War II fame. Here pilot Tony LeVier banks around a pylon as he qualified his P-38 Lightning at 376.438 miles an hour for the Thompson Trophy Race in 1946. (Plain Dealer)

CHARLES A. OTIS, prominent financier and businessman who was dubbed "Mr. Cleveland" for his civic contributions, plays the role of greeter during one of the city's sesquicentennial events in 1946. The clothes horse he is welcoming is one of Cleveland's most famous sons, Leslie Townes Hope, also known in pugilistic circles as Packy East, and in show business circles as Bob Hope. (WRHS)

THE SESQUICENTENNIAL CELEBRATION included the help of visiting celebrities in the planting of a tree as part of an overall effort to restore the city to its former place as "The Forest City." Among those in 1946 who helped were Jimmy Durante and Garry Moore, posing with the shovel. Behind Durante is Charles A. Otis, prominent Cleveland financier, while the city's shade-tree commissioner, Edward Scanlon, stands bemused off to the left. (WRHS)

CLEVELAND'S STRENGTH is under its bridges, in the industrial Cuyahoga Valley, as this photograph by William A. Wynne suggests. One of the long freighters from the Great Lakes is moving up-
river, laden with iron ore, heading for one of the steel mills. The view is from the old Superior Viaduct
looking southeast towards the Detroit-Superior High Level Bridge. (Plain Dealer)

[133]

LOOKING DOWN on the central area of
downtown Cleveland from a Goodyear
blimp on a sunny June afternoon in
1947. (Plain Dealer)

TWO OF CLEVELAND'S BEST-KNOWN SYM-bols, the Terminal Tower and the statue of the city's greatest mayor, Tom L. Johnson, come together in this photograph by Perry Cragg taken in 1946. (News)

PROMOTER BILL VEECK, who blazed across the Cleveland sports scene like a meteor after World War II, proudly holds up Bob Feller's new $80,000 contract. It was a sensational sum in the sports world of 1947. (Plain Dealer)

ELIOT NESS, Cleveland's famous "Untouchable," lifts his hand in greeting in the right foreground during his campaign for mayor in 1947. Judge Victor Cohen is in the rear. Ness, the Republican candidate, lost the election. It was his last hurrah in Cleveland politics. (Cragg)

SHORTLY AFTER LARRY DOBY, the first black baseball player in the American League, joined the Cleveland Indians in mid-summer of 1947, photographer Herman Seid played a hunch and waited in the stadium's parking lot for a scene that he figured would be inevitable—the youthful quest for autographs. It worked out even better than he had hoped, as shown by this picture of Doby in flight and the crowd of kids in pursuit. (Seid)

"ONE OF MY BEST"

THE OUTSTANDING HERO of the Cleveland Indians team that won the 1948 American League pennant and then went on to beat the Boston Braves in the World Series was player-manager Lou Boudreau. Everybody agreed that the way he played in the field and hit the baseball made him the best manager in baseball that year. (Seid)

[135]

THE CLIMAX of the thrilling 1948 baseball season was the World Series playoff against the Boston Braves. The crowds that gathered to watch the games in Municipal Stadium set new baseball attendance records. This aerial view shows the many thousands of fans hustling down the West Ninth Street ramp towards the stadium. (Seid)

MOVIE STAR JAMES STEWART shields his eyes as he follows the overhead action at the 1948 National Air Races. To Stewart's left is film actress Dorothy Hart of Cleveland; to his right is Allen J. Lowe, then general manager of the Carter Hotel. (Plain Dealer)

TRAGEDY: AN F-51 racer piloted by William P. Odom crashed into the home of the Bradley C. Laird family in the small city of Berea, just south of Cleveland Airport, during the 1949 National Air Races. The wrecked home, saturated with aviation gasoline, is shown burning minutes after the crash in which the pilot and two members of the Laird family, mother and baby, were killed. Neighbors are trying to retrieve some of the Laird furniture from the flames. (Plain Dealer)

THE SWEETEST VICTORY OF ALL: After winning the championship of the All-America Conference four years in a row, 1946-1949, and compiling an unbelievable record of 52 wins and only 4 losses, the Cleveland Browns in 1950 joined the National Football League to face their biggest test. Their debut, in a contest that matched them against the defending NFL champions, the Philadelphia Eagles, was sensational. They beat the Eagles, 35 to 10. At the end of the game, Otto Graham, the Brown's star quarterback, was awarded the Robert French Memorial Trophy as the most valuable player in the opening game. He had passed for three toughdowns and had scored a fourth himself. He and Coach Brown are obvious in their pleasure as they hold the trophy for a photographer. (News)

EUCLID AVENUE AND PUBLIC SQUARE looked this way on a sunny summer's day in 1948 before the streetcars, downtown movie theaters, and other familiar institutions of the prewar city gave way to postwar progress. (Cragg)

A NIGHTTIME SCENE along the Cleveland waterfront, looking south towards downtown, as captured by photographer William A. Ashbolt in the early 1950s. (Plain Dealer)

ONE OF THE HEAVIEST SNOWFALLS in Cleveland history descended on the city in late November 1950, and its effect is clearly scene in this photograph *(below)* of Euclid Avenue near East Seventy-seventh Street. Vehicular traffic, including streetcars, was brought to a standstill by the blizzard. The church on the left, the Second Church of Christ, Scientist, later became the 77th Street Theater of the Cleveland Play House. The same blizzard was just beginning to get its second blustery breath at the moment the picture above was taken at the corner of East Sixth Street and Superior Avenue, close to the venerable Hotel Hollenden that stood on that corner at the time. Clevelanders who remember it will get nostalgic over the name, Sammy Watkins Orchestra, on the marquee. Sammy held the record for playing the Vogue Room. One of his vocalists earlier had been Dean Martin. (Seid)

[139]

UP WEST THIRD STREET from the Cleveland lakefront near Municipal Stadium, on a bright summer's day in about 1950: The scene was photographed by Marvin Greene. (Plain Dealer)

Index

Academy, 21
Allen Theater, 93, 107
Allerton, Robert, 60
Andorn, Sid, 118
Andrews, Clark & Company, 26
Andrews' Folly, 41
Andrews, Samuel, 41
Angle, 33
Arcade, 53
Armory, 87
Armour's Saloon, Ross, 75
Ashbolt, William A., 138
Astor family, 86
Ayres, Col. Leonard P., 95

Baker, Mayor Newton D., 84, 87
Ball, Ernest Roland, 59
Ball, Mrs. Ernest Roland (Maud), 59
Barry, Edwin, 102
Bedford, 85
Benny, Jack, 116
Berea, 136
Biggar, Dr. H. F., 72
B'nai Jeshurun, 70
Boardman, will, 48
Bolster, Lieutenant, 105
Boudreau, Lou, 135
Bratenahl, 57, 59
Brickels, John, 130
Brighton (South Brooklyn), 17
Broadway Market, Lower, 56
Brooklyn Heights, 17
Brooklyn Township, 16
Brookside Park, 121
Brookside Zoo, 97
Brown, Coach Paul, 130, 136
Brush, Charles F., 36, 40
Burke Lakefront Airport, 52
Burke, Mayor Thomas A., 129

Burton, Mayor E., 124
Burton, U.S. Sen. Harold H., 129
Butler, Bernie, 9
Butt, Major, 74

C & B Line (Cleveland-Buffalo steamer line), 106
Carroll, Gene, 109
Carter Hotel, 136
Carter, Maj. Lorenzo, 15, 16, 17
Case Block, 23, 35, 64, 81
Case, George, 122
Case, Leonard, Sr., 20, 23
Case School of Applied Science, 20
Case-Western Reserve University, 20
Central High School, 26
Central Viaduct, 52
Chadwick, Mrs. Cassie L. "the Duchess of Diamonds," 65
Chapman, Ray, 86
Chessie System, 9
Chisholm, William, 43
City Hall, 35, 36, 54, 56, 63, 64, 81, 120
City of Cleveland (airplane), 96
City of Cleveland III (steamer), 106
City of Erie (steamer), 106
City of Ohio, *see* Ohio City
Clark, David, 15
Cleaveland, Gen. Moses, 12, 13, 14, 38, 94, 126
Clement, William, 16
Cleveland Association of Colored Men, 80
Cleveland Automobile Club, 9, 58

Cleveland Baseball Company, 110
Cleveland Board of Education, 56, 110
Cleveland Browns (football team), 130, 136
Cleveland centennial celebration, 36, 54
Cleveland Chamber of Commerce, 61, 96, 108
Cleveland Clinic, 100, 101
Cleveland College, 108
Cleveland, Columbus & Cincinnati Railroad, 24
Cleveland Electric Illumination Company, 40, 74, 95
Cleveland Evening Post, 62
Cleveland Fire Department, 30, 68, 69, 100, 110, 112
Cleveland Gas & Coke Company, 53
Cleveland Grays, 21, 32
Cleveland Heights, 57
Cleveland Herald, 23
Cleveland Hopkins International Airport, 105
Cleveland House, 38
Cleveland Indians (baseball team), 86, 109, 111, 116, 130, 135
Cleveland Institute of Music, 43
Cleveland Iron Company, 24
Cleveland Iron Mining Company, 24
Cleveland Leader, 23, 45, 67
Cleveland Municipal Airport, 103, 104, 105, 113
Cleveland Municipal Stadium, 93, 111, 114, 116, 119, 130, 135, 140
Cleveland Museum of Art, 42, 91, 116

Cleveland News, 9, 67, 111, 128
Cleveland Plain Dealer, 9, 23, 34, 48, 58, 62, 64, 67, 83, 90, 97, 111
Cleveland Playhouse, 139
Cleveland Police Department, 42, 61, 62, 87, 94, 97
Cleveland, Pres. Grover, 38
Cleveland Press, 9, 67, 92, 111
Cleveland Public Auditorium, 56, 87, 115, 120
Cleveland Public Library, 9, 57, 81, 83, 93
Cleveland Railway Company, 96
Cleveland Rams (football team), 124
Cleveland sesquicentennial celebration, 132
Cleveland Symphony Orchestra, 116
Cleveland Trade Aircraft School, 126
Cleveland Transit System, 96
Cleveland Trust Company Bank, 51, 85
Cleveland Veterans' Volunteer Brigade, 44
Cleveland Yacht Club, 70
Cobb, Florence, 60
Cobbledick, Gordon, 111
Cohen, Judge Victor, 134
Cole, Kenneth R., 96
Collinwood, 68, 69
Commercial Bank of Lake Erie, 20
Conkright, Red, 130
Conneaut, 12
Connecticut (state), 11, 12
Connecticut Land Company, 12, 13
Coogan, Jackie, 91
Coolidge, Pres. Calvin, 90
Country Club, 48
Cragg, Perry, 111, 134
Crawford, Federick C., 113
Crittendon Home, 34
Crowell, Ben, 48
Cummings, Lt. C. M., 104
Curtiss, Glenn, 70
Cuyahoga Building, 32
Cuyahoga County Court House, 23, 27, 45, 56, 78
Cuyahoga County Morgue, 101

D & C Line (Detroit-Cleveland steamer line), 106
Davenport, Homer, 61
Davey, Gov. Martin L., 115
Davis, Gov. Harry L., 81, 114
Dead River & Ohio Mining Company, 24

Detroit-Superior High-Level Bridge, 78, 80, 96, 133
Doby, Larry, 135
Dolinger, Milton, 9
Donahey, Hal, 90
Doolittle, Gen. James, 102, 104
Dragonette, Jessica, 115
Dunham House, 38
Dunn, Danny, 118
Dunn Field, 110
Dunn, Jimmy, 75
Durante, Jimmy, 132

East Cleveland, 39, 57
East Ohio Gas Company, 53, 127
East Side, 69, 78, 116, 127
Eaton, Cyrus S., 67, 72
Eaton, Rev. Charles A., 67, 72
Eckener, Dr. Hugo, 105
Edgewater Bath House, 83, 87
Edgewater Park, 83, 84
Eisenmann, John M., 53
Eldridge, David, 15
Ellington Apartments, 112
Empire Burlesque Theater, 98
Epworth Methodist Church, 116
Erie Canal (Ohio-Erie Canal), 18, 19, 20, 21, 35
Erieview Urban Renewal, 101
Euclid, 69
Euclid Avenue Baptist Church, 67, 72, 73
Euclid Beach, 70, 90
Everett, Sylvester, 43
Exposition Hall, 56

Federal Building, 23, 35, 49, 57, 64, 101
Federal Public Works Program, 12
Feller, Bob, 130, 134
Ferrell, Wesley, 111
First Methodist Church, 51
First Presbyterian Church, 21, 23
First Trinity Episcopal Church, 51
Fiske, John, 26
Five-Mile Crib, 80
Flats, 15, 22, 24, 25, 29, 46, 70, 86
Forest City Club, 26
Forest City House, 22, 30, 37, 38
Forest City Railway, 62
Forest Hill, 26, 39, 57, 72, 73
Founders Day, 36, 86, 126
Four-in-Hand & Tandem Club, 59
Franco-Prussian War (victory celebration), 33

Gardner, Nancy, 9
Garfield, Pres. James A., 36
Gates Mills, 57
George, David Lloyd, prime minister of England, 84
Gildersleeve, Clifford, 96
Gompers, Samuel, 81
Goode, Prof. J. Paul, 93
Gordon Park, 49
Grabenstetter, Mary Jane, 9
Graham, Otto, 136
Grand Army of the Republic, 60
Graney, Jack, 109
Graul, Police Chief Jacob, 94
Great Lakes Exposition, 93, 119, 120
Greene, Marvin, 140
Group Plan (downtown development), 56
Guthrie, Thomas, 9

Haberton, John, 16
Hale, W. B., 46
Hanna, Dan R., Sr., 59
Hanna, Howard M., 59, 60
Hanna, Mrs. Howard M., 60
Hanna, Ruth (Mrs. Medill McCormack), 60, 61
Hanna, Sen. Marcus Alonzo, 55, 60, 61
Hanna Theater, 93
Hart, Dorothy, 136
Hayes, Patrick Cardinal, 115
Hay, Sec. of State John, 43, 61
Heisler, Fritz, 130
Henie, Sonja, 118
Herbert, Gov. Thomas J., 104
Herrick, Ambassador Myron T., 74
Higbee Company, 34, 37, 88
Holden, A. F. (Burt), 59
Holden, L. Dean, 48, 59
Hollenden Hotel, 64, 67, 139
Holley, John Milton, 14
Holm, Eleanor, 120
Hope, Bob (Leslie Townes Hope; also "Packy East"), 124
Hopkins, City Mgr. William R., 105
Hoyt, James H., 59
Hunter, Pinky, 108
Huron Road Hospital, 97

Illuminating Company, 40, 74, 95
Inches, Chloe (Mrs. William Clement), 16

John Carroll University, 102
Johnson, Levi, 17

Johnson, Mayor Tom L., 43, 46, 55, 56, 62, 63, 64, 134
Jones Building, 35

Kalish, Max, 110
Kelley, Alfred, 16, 17, 18, 24
Kelley Block, 45
Kilbane, Johnny, 75
King, Adm. Ernest J., 129
Kingsbury, James, 16
Kinsbury Run, 32
Kirtland, Turhand, 15
Kobel, Hans, 88
Kohler, Mayor Fred, 61, 63, 74
Kraffert, Andrew J., 72, 97
Kresge store, S. S., 69

Laird family, Bradley C., 136
Lakeside Hospitals, 52
Lake Theater, 93
Lakeview Cemetery, 26, 36, 68
Lakeview Elementary School, 68
Lakeview Park, 78
Lakewood, 17, 57
Landon, Alfred, gov. of Kansas, 117
Landon, Joseph, 14
Lausche, Gov. Frank J., 129
Leader Building, 51
League Park, 110
LeVier, Tony, 132
Liederkranz Hall, 66
Lighthouse, 17, 18, 31, 37
Lincoln, Pres. Abraham, 28, 29, 110
Lindbergh, Charles A., 102, 104
Linndale, 17
Little, Bascom, 60
Losteiner, George (Jiggs), 85
Louis, Joe, 116
Lowe, Allen J., 136
Luna Park, 102
Lyon Tailors (baseball team), 121

McBride, Arthur B. (Mickey), 130
McCormack, Col. Robert, 60
McCormack, Medill, 60, 61
McCurdy, Miss Lucia (Mrs. Malcolm L. McBride), 60
Mack, Connie, 109
McKinley, Pres. William F., 55, 60, 61
McNamee, Graham, 109
McNichols, Walter, 111
Manning, Tom (Red), 109
Marine Hospital, 23
Maroni, Louis, 50
Marshall, Mayor John D., 102

Martin Company, Glenn L., 96, 113
Martin, Dean, 139
Martin, Glenn L., 104
Matowitz, Police Chief George J., 115
May Company, 28
Merritt, E. A., 59
Methodist Church, 33
Millionaires' Row, 43, 51
Misch, Richard, 9
Moore, Garry, 132
Morgan, Garrett, 80
Motley, Marion, 130
Mowrey's Tavern, 38
Murway, Alfred K., 9

National Air Races, 93, 103, 104, 105, 113, 132, 136
National Eucharistic Congress, 93, 114, 115
Ness, Eliot, 134
Newburgh, 32
Newburgh & Kinsman Line, 32
Newburgh Township, 16
Niagara, Chief Ghema, 126
Novotney, E. Ladislaw, 12

Odom, William P., 136
Ohio & Erie Canal, see Erie Canal
Ohio Bell Telephone Company, 45, 66, 98
Ohio City, 16, 17, 19, 21, 44
Old Stone Church, 21, 23, 34, 45
Omaha Club Dance Hall, 66
O'Mick, John, 16
Oswald, W. G., 126
Otis, Charles A., 59, 132
Owens, Jesse, 122, 123
Owens, Mrs. Jesse (Ruth), 122

Paar, Jack, 124
Painter, Kenyon, 48
Palace Theater, 93
Parch, Miss Grace, 9
Patterson, J. M., 60
Patterson, Miss Eleanor (Countess Gizycka), 60
Peake, George, 16
Pease, Seth, 13, 14
"Pease's Hotel," 16
Perkins Beach, 108
Perkins, Jacob B., 59
Perry, Commodore Oliver Hazard, 29, 49
Perry Monument, Commodore, 18, 29, 33, 49
Pershing, Gen. John J., 87
Pike, Kermit, 9

Playhouse Square, 93, 107
Porter, Augustus, 14
Poschke Barbecues (baseball team), 121
Public Square, 16, 17, 18, 20, 21, 22, 23, 26, 27, 28, 29, 30, 33, 35, 36, 37, 38, 40, 45, 49, 50, 54, 56, 60, 61, 62, 65, 88, 93, 95, 108, 137

Raymond, Samuel, 51
Republican Party national conventions, 89, 93, 117
Republic Steel Corporation, 118
Reservoir Walk, 33
Rice, Harvey, 18
Rice, W. L., 59
Risko, Johnny, 118
Robertson, Carl T., 64
Rockefeller & Andrews, 29
Rockefeller Building, 41
Rockefeller, John D., 26, 29, 39, 41, 46, 67, 72, 73, 124
Rockefeller, Mrs. John D., 72
Rockefeller, William Avery, 26
Rocky River (town), 31, 57
Rocky River Reservation, 85
Roosevelt, Alice (Mrs. Nicholas Longworth), 60
Roosevelt, Pres. Franklin D., 113, 117
Roosevelt, Pres. Theodore, 60, 61
Rose, Billy, 120
Rowell, Glenn, 109
Rowland, Paul, 9
Royon, Miss Betty, 9

Saint John's Cathedral, 53, 86, 92, 115
Saint John's Episcopal Church, 33, 44
Saint Malachi's Catholic Church, 33, 39
Saint Paul's Church, 60
Saint Theodosius Church (Greek Orthodox), 125
Sammy Watkins Orchestra, 139
Scanlon, Edward, 132
Schmidt, Max, 88
Schmidt, Mrs. Max, 88
Schmunk, R. J., 58
Schofield Building, 50
Schofield, Levi T., 50
Schrembs, Bishop John, 115
Second Church of Christ Scientist, 139
Second Presbyterian Church, 32
Seeandbee (steamer), 106
Seid, Herman, 9, 103, 108, 135

Seneca, Chief, 16
Settlers Landing, 14
77th Street Theater, 139
Severance Hall, 116
Seymour, Belden, 59
Shaker Heights, 56, 67
Shepard, Theodore, 14
Sheraton-Cleveland Hotel, 22, 30
Sietman, Mrs. Adeline, 126
Silverthorn Inn, 31
Smith, Alfred E., gov. of New York, 115
Smith, George H., 53
Smith, Msgr. Joseph F., 115
Society for Savings Building, 34, 45
Sohm, Ed, 66
Sohm, George, 66
Soldiers' Aid Society, 30
Soldiers & Sailors Monument, 18, 49, 50
South Brooklyn (Brighton), 17
Spafford, Maj. Amos, 14, 15
Speaker, Tris, 130
Standard Oil Company (Sohio), 9, 26, 46, 71
State Theater, 93
Stewart, James, 136
Stiles, Charles Phelps, 15
Stiles, Job Phelps, 14, 15
Stiles, Tabitha Cumi (Mrs. Job Phelps Stiles), 14, 15
Stillman Hotel, 42
Stillman Theater, 42, 93
Stockly, John G., 22
Stockly's Pier, 22
Stoddard, Richard M., 14
Stow, Joshua, 14
Sullivan, Dr. R. P., 115
Superior Railway Company, 40
Superior Viaduct, 39, 78, 80, 133

Taft, Pres. William Howard, 74
Taylor, Dan, 111
Terminal Tower, see Union Terminal
Thompson, Craig, 9
Thompson Products Company, 113
Townes, Mayor Clayton, 91
Trinity Church, 21
Trinity Episcopal Cathedral, 72
Tripolsky, Mrs. Estelle, 126
Turner, Col. Roscoe C., 113

Union Passenger Station, 30
Union Terminal, 30, 56, 87, 88, 93, 98, 99, 107, 134
University Circle, 116
U.S. centennial celebration, 38
U.S. Post Office, 35, 49

Vail, Thomas, 9
Van Sweringen, M. J., 30, 56, 87, 98
Van Sweringen, O. P., 30, 56, 87, 98
Veeck, Bill, 134
Vogue Room, 139
Voights, Bob, 130

Wade, Jeptha H., 42
Wade, Jeptha H., II, 42
Wade Park, 42
Wallace, Fire Chief George A., 110
Walworth, Judge, 17
Wardin, Miss Peggy, 9
Warren, Moses, Jr., 14
WCLE-Radio, 109
Weddell House, 28, 41
Weissmueller, Johnny, 120
West Cleveland, 17
Western Reserve Historical Society, 9

Western Reserve of Connecticut, 11, 12, 13, 14, 16
Western Union Telegraph Company, 42
Westlake Hotel, 31
West Side, 16, 21, 39, 78, 83, 108
West Side Market, 100, 131
West Third Street Bridge, 76
WEWS-TV, 41
WGAR-Radio, 125
White Autos (baseball team), 121
White Motor Corporation, 9
White Sewing Machine Company, 57, 58
White Stanhope Steamer, 58
White Steam Car, 57
White, Will, 59
WHK-Radio, 88, 95, 109
Wilk, Charles, 111
William H. Mack (steamer), 76
Williams, Lt. Al, 102
Wilson, Pres. Woodrow, 87
Winslow, Richard, 28
Winton (automobile), 62, 65
Winton, Alexander, 55, 65
Witt, Peter, 63
WTAM-Radio, 105, 109
Wynne, William A., 133

York, Robert H., 48
York, Roy, 48
Young, Denton True (Cy), 130

Zephyr (boat), 17